Valerie Meyer

Candle-making is fun

Chock-a-block full of ideas and easy instructions — for the whole family

J L van Schaik

Contents

Acknowledgements

I would like to express my gratitude to many people without whose contribution this book probably would never have materialized. Firstly my family who have always encouraged and supported me and especially my two sons. Reinier actually discovered the hand-moulding method of candle making and Etienne is a keen hand-moulder.

My gratitude also extends to the Craftywax Club Teachers and their club members whose enthusiasm and creativity have resulted in many of the candle-making ideas featured in this book. I would further like to thank my sister, Patricia Margetts, for her help.

Published by J.L. van Schaik (Pty) Ltd, 1064 Arcadia Street, Hatfield, Pretoria
All rights reserved
Copyright: © 1990 Valerie Meyer

No part of this book may be reproduced or transmitted in any form or by any electronic or mechanical means, including photocopying and recording, or by any information storage or retrieval system, without written permission from the publisher.

First published 1990
ISBN 0 627 01725 8

Cover design by Dirk Büchner
Photographer: Bert Jeltsema
Illustrations: Sigi Dannheimer
Typeset in 10.6 on 12 pt Caxton Light by Reprotype
Printed and bound by National Book Printers, Goodwood, Cape

Introduction	1
What you will need	4
Before you begin	5
Hints	5
About colour	8
About fragrance	8
Floating candles	9
Perfumed floating candles	9
Flower-shaped floating candles	12
Outdoor floating candles	12
Large outdoor floating candles	12
Garden Candles	13
Garden candle with large outdoor floating candle 'top'	16
Garden candle with a ball candle nestling in a wax bowl	16
Wax bowls	17
Exotic flower candles	20
Wax leaves	20
Candles in chocolate moulds	21
Improvised moulds	25
Candles made using improvised moulds	28
Large candles made in improvised moulds	29
Dipped candles	32
Hand-moulded candles	33
Hand-moulded beetle	36
Tomato candles	36
Russian doll candles	36
Owls	36
Wonderworm candle	36
Pumpkin	40
Spider	41
Snail	41
Mushroom	44
Panther	44
Cat	44
Bird	44
Ghosts	45
Decorating candles	46
Painting	46
Wax appliqué	46
Pressed flowers	47
Cutting shapes into a candle	47
Completing decorated candles	47
Angel's wings candles	48
Layered candles	49
Sand and glue container candles	50
Buyer's guide	52
Patterns for exotic flower candles	52

Introduction

Before the invention of the paraffin lamp and the electric globe, candles were used for lighting and were made either from animal fat or beeswax. These candles were merely functional and, also because of the crude materials used, not very decorative. The paraffin waxes available today are however of superior quality and candle making has become a very rewarding art form and in my case, quite addictive!

The success of candle making lies in the correct wax formula and it took many costly experiments on my part to establish the most effective formulation. This book is based on the use of ready formulated waxes of which *Craftywax* is currently the only one on the market.

Today candles are used mostly on special occasions for creating various atmospheres ranging from tranquillity to romance or simply fun. As such, candles contribute much to successful entertaining, of which the following are a few examples.

Outdoor entertaining

On warm summer nights an exotic mood can be created outside by using perfumed flower candles, wax leaves and wax bowls with candles floating on the swimming pool, sand candles displayed on the patio, or garden candles set amongst the plants. A humorous touch is added by animal candles lurking on the ground or perched on bamboo sticks.

A seafood table

Combine shells and bits of seaweed with your shell candles for a different centrepiece on the dinner table.

Cheese and wine party

Imaginative use can be made of fruit, vegetables and various candles to create a mellow mood.

Birthday parties

This provides much scope for creativity, depending on the age and interests of the person whose birthday is celebrated. For a young girl's party flower floating candles, ball candles and wax bowls can be used to great effect, especially if combined with interesting holders such as overturned, decorated champagne glasses. Children can help to make candles for their own parties.

A ghostly feast

Adults and children can all join in the fun of making ghosts, spiders, pumpkins and bats. And what better atmosphere at night than that provided by flickering candles casting weird and wonderful shadows!

Christmas time

Wreaths and Santa Clauses on the mantelpiece and dinner table, and angel's wings candles placed near the Christmas tree ... these also make treasured handmade gifts. Children can hand-mould their favourite animals as gifts for their favourite people.

Candles as gifts

A gift of candles is always well received by friends and acquaintances alike and may be given instead of flowers on any occasion. Candles also make excellent fête items and because they are easy to make, children can help. The most popular gift items are the perfumed floating candles because they are small and affordable. Packaging of any gift is of course very important and you have a wide choice of boxes, baskets, cellophane wrapping or bags (obtainable in various sizes from most confectioners), and even cloth such as tulle or linen.

There are endless possibilities for creativity in candle making and the purpose of this book is to present this art in an enjoyable and easy manner which would appeal to adults and children alike. May they all experience the pleasure of making and using candles.

1 *What you will need (see page 4).*

2 *Making candles – Etienne Meyer, Louise Müller, Janine Müller and Valerie Meyer.*

3 *Entertaining with candles.*

4 *Exotic flower candles (p. 20).*

3

4

3

What you will need

Craftywax basic candle-making kit

The kit contains:
1. Interior wax
2. Exterior wax
3. Colour chips
4. Wick and
5. Candle perfume.

It contains enough materials to make approximately 40 floating candles or numerous other candles. These candle-making kits are available in three basic colour groups:

(a) Red label — white, pink or red candles and rose perfume.
(b) Blue label — white, light blue, dark blue or green candles and hyacinth perfume.
(c) Yellow label — white, lemon, yellow or orange candles and linden blossom perfume.

N.B. All the waxes, perfumes, wick and colour chips mentioned in this book are also available separately. (See buyer's guide on p. 52.)

Craftywax glossy sealer — not included in the kit. (Is only required if candles are to be decorated.)

Electric stove — your kitchen stove can be protected by foil if you do not have a hot plate. If only a gas stove is available, ensure that the wax is melted at a low temperature, as high heat can damage the wax. Also see that there is no wax on the outside of the container you are using.

Kettle or jug for melting and pouring wax.

Dipping pots which may be old pots or simply large tins.

Baking sheet with a depth of at least 17 mm.

Tart dish for making angel's wings candles.

Wax wrap, foil, tissue paper and newspaper.

A makeshift washing line to be used for floating candles.

Tins, lids, bowls and dishes to be used as moulds or for mixing wax (stirring).

Chocolate moulds are very handy, especially different-sized ball and egg shapes.

Cutters (cookie and icing) — various shapes of cookie cutters may be used for floating candles while the icing cutters are used mainly for wax appliqué work.

Thermometer — a candy thermometer that measures up to 150°C or more will be suitable. If you do not have a thermometer you will know that the temperature of the *Interior* or *Exterior* wax is

- 60°C when it resembles cream
- 90°C when it resembles milk
- *Too hot* to work with when it resembles water.

Kitchen utensils such as a wooden spoon for stirring, small sharp knife (with smooth, not serrated edge), sosatie sticks, and even clothes pegs.

General household items such as scissors, darning needles, Prestik, paper glue (liquid clear glue) and poster paints.

Soldering iron to be used in wax appliqué work and should be 25 W.

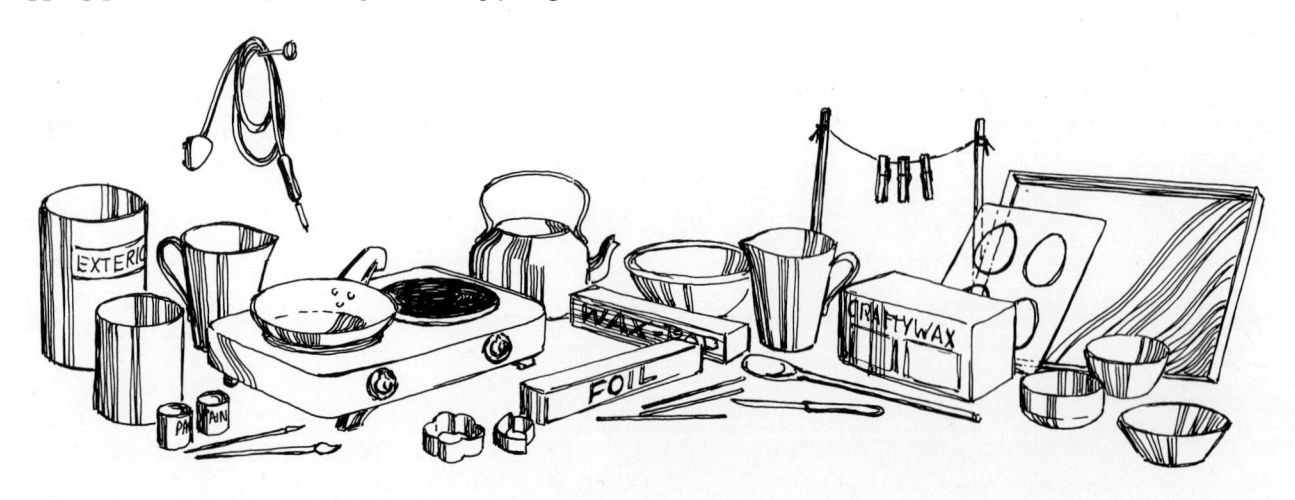

Before you begin

1. Candle making is a suitable craft for *children*, but only when *assisted by an adult*. A formulated wax (such as *Craftywax*) seldom requires high temperatures. However, when working with temperatures above 95°C such as in the case of *Glossy Sealer Wax*, which is used at 103°C, it is essential that you use a thermometer.

2. The basic safety principles which apply to the use of cooking oil also apply to wax, although the required working temperatures for wax are not nearly as high as those of oil. The following rules should be strictly adhered to:

    (a) *Melt wax over low heat and stir frequently* to distribute the heat evenly. Too high temperatures will not only be dangerous but will damage the molecular structure of the wax.

    (b) *Never leave wax unattended on the stove.* In the event of the wax catching fire, simply smother the flames with a lid or damp cloth. *(Do not douse flames with water.)*

    (c) When pouring wax always use a paper towel to *wipe wax from the utensil* so that wax does not end up on the stove and cause trouble.

    (d) *Never leave wax to set in a kettle, jug or dipping pot after use.* Pour the melted wax into a dish and chop it up when it is cool, or pour the wax into a baking sheet and cut it up while still warm (store wax in labelled plastic bags when cool and simply melt again when required). Melting wax which has set in a pot is dangerous if you put this pot on the stove because the wax at the bottom will melt and overheat while the wax at the top remains solid: The pressure that builds up may shoot the wax upwards out of the pot.

    (e) *Never leave a burning candle unattended.*

Hints

1. Cover working surfaces with old newspapers or wax wrap and the stove with tin foil to facilitate quick and easy cleaning.

2. Save scraps of wax as well as used candles for making outdoor sand candles.

3. Should you experience difficulty in getting a candle out of a mould simply put it in the fridge for a few minutes.

4. Never give up on a candle because

    (a) you can fill up cracks and gaps with wax that has cooled to a gelled state;
    (b) the candle will be covered by *Exterior* wax anyway and
    (c) it can be smoothed by the *Glossy Sealer* wax.

5. Objects which can be used instead of candle holders are:

    (a) Sheets of glass which can be cut into the desired shape and size by your local glass dealer (see p. 22).
    (b) Champagne glasses (the wide type) (see p. 23).
    (c) Leaves (especially banana leaves) will protect your table from any wax dripping;
    (d) A variety of bowls, etc. for the floating candles.

6. Do not extinguish a candle by blowing out the flame, but rather snuff it out and your candle will burn better the next time.

7. Be careful of wax dripping on paving because this is very difficult to remove.

8. Wax may be removed from a table cloth by

    (a) rubbing until the wax flakes and falls off;
    (b) thereafter ironing between two sheets of brown paper; and
    (c) if necessary using a stain remover such as *Shout* or *Preen*.

5 Wax bowl (p. 17) with outdoor floating candle (p. 12).

6 Hanging wax bowl (p. 17) with perfumed floating candle (p. 9).

7 Seafood table with angel's wings candle (p. 48), shell candles (p. 21) and free form sand and glue candle (p. 50).

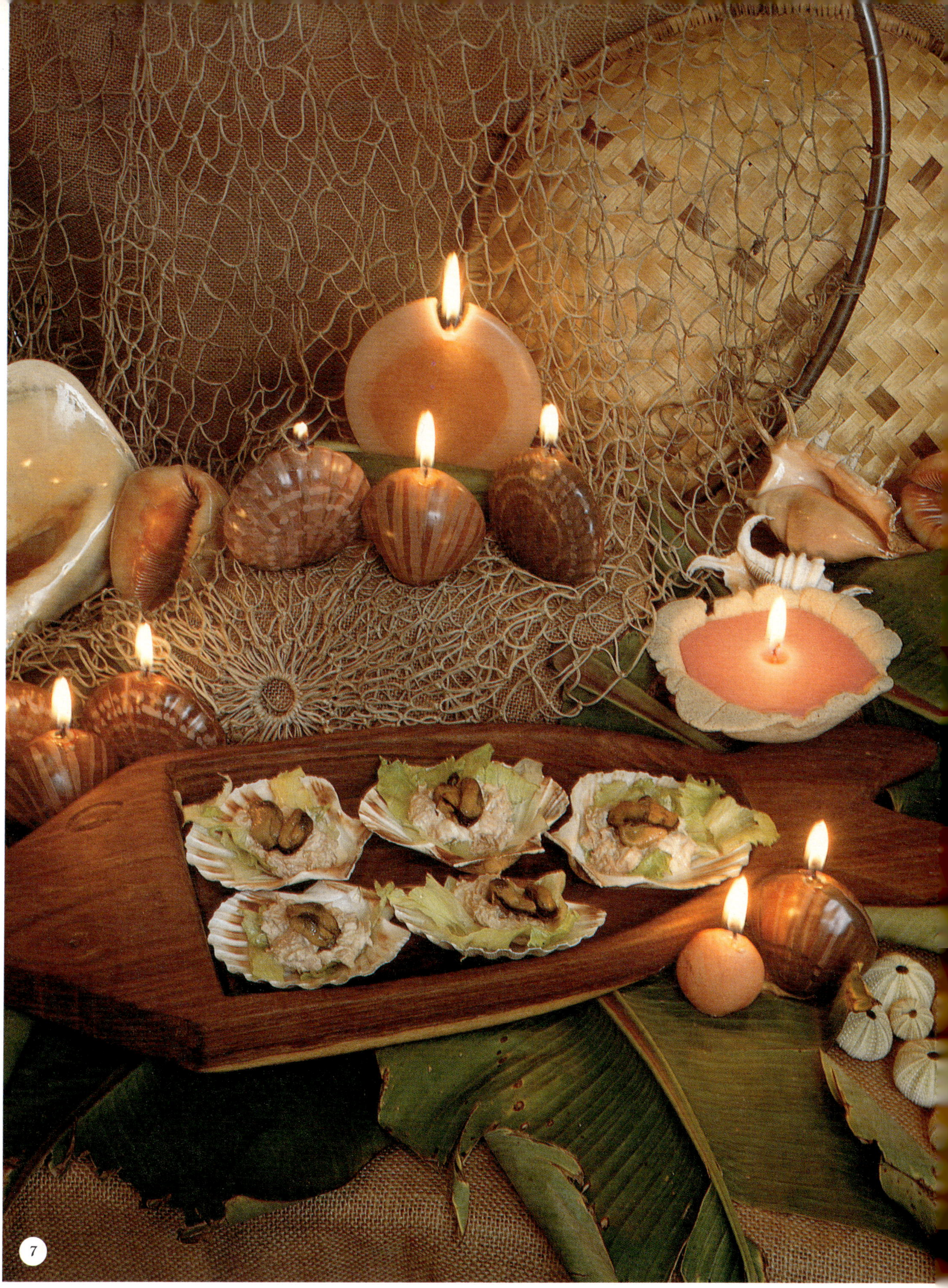
7

About colour

To mix colours, use this very basic guide (you can cut the colour chips into pieces):

White	–	No colour is required
Deep red	–	Red colour chip
Cherry red	–	Red with just a tiny bit of yellow
Pink	–	Use a piece of red colour chip. The more you use the darker it will be.
Wine red	–	Red and a tiny bit of blue
Dusty pink	–	The same combination as above but in much smaller quantities.
Yellow	–	Yellow colour chip
Lemon	–	Just a little yellow
Honey	–	Yellow, little blue and red
Brown	–	Yellow, blue and red
Black	–	Black colour chip
Orange	–	Yellow and red
Blue	–	Blue colour chip but use small pieces for light blue
Green	–	Blue and yellow
Turquoise	–	Blue with a tiny bit of yellow
Purple	–	Blue and red
Lilac	–	As above but in smaller quantities

N.B. *To test the colour of the wax, dip a block of wax into the melted coloured wax and leave to cool completely before checking what the final colour will be.*

Do not add too much colour; rather use smaller pieces of colour chip at a time because you can always add more.

About fragrance

Do not use potpourri basic oils which will disturb the balance of the wax formulations, but do make use of the proper candle fragrances to add the final touches to your candles. The candles will not only have visual but also sensory appeal and will neutralise household odours and smoke when burning.

A simple guide as to which fragrances match the different colours is as follows:

White	– Lily of the valley
Red and pink	– Rose, tea rose or carnation
Yellow and orange	– Honeysuckle, freesia
Black and browns	– Wild orchid
Blue, green, purple, etc.	– Lavender, hyacinth, violet

Floating candles

Perfumed floating candles

These candles are not only economical but also versatile in that they can be used with virtually any theme. They also make the most popular gifts. They can be made in any shape (heart, round, flower, diamond, star, etc.) but should have a diameter of approximately 5 cm and a thickness of 1,5 cm to ensure a burning time of approximately two to three hours. (Make your shapes thicker if a longer burning time is required.)

To use these candles simply fill any receptacle with water and gently place the floating candle on the water and light. Flowers may be floated with these candles.

Step 1
Place *Interior* wax in kettle and *Exterior* wax in dipping pot. Heat over very low heat. Stir wax frequently to distribute heat evenly.

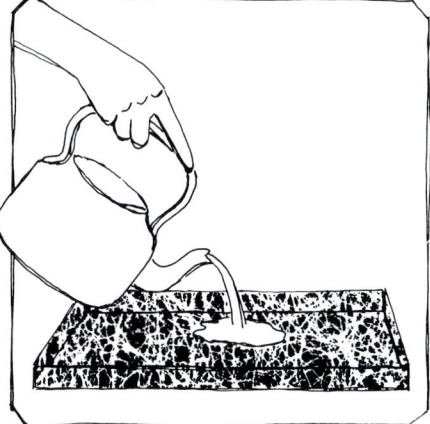

Step 2
When *Interior* was reaches 60°C (use thermometer), pour into a small baking sheet until filled to the brim.

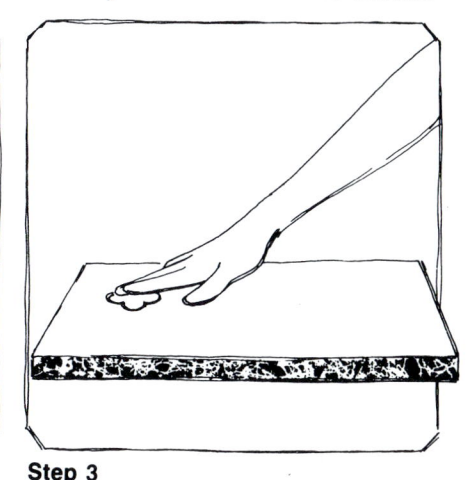

Step 3
Leave wax in baking sheet to cool (approx. 45 min.). When wax has set but is still warm, cut out with a cookie cutter.

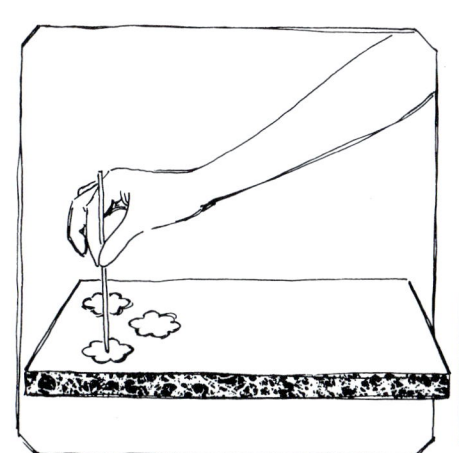

Step 4
Pierce holes in the middle of each candle, using the flat end of a sosatie stick. Leave candles in baking sheet to cool completely. Remove surrounding wax and store for re-use.

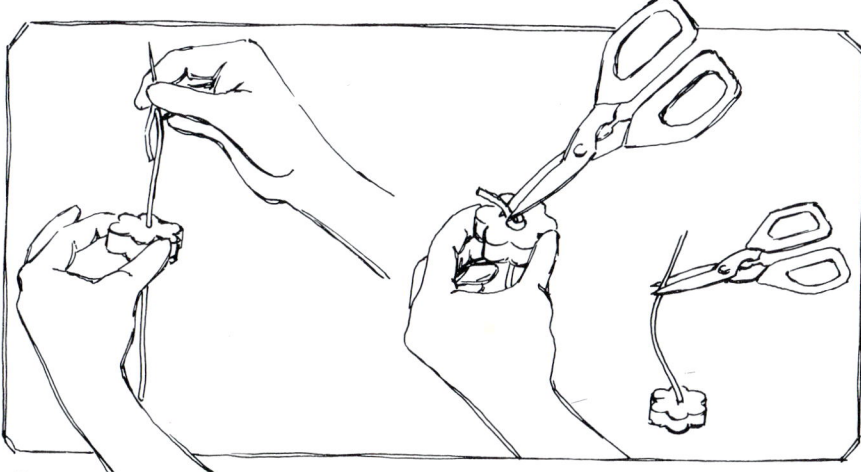

Step 5
(a) Using an embroidery needle, thread wick into candles.
(b) Knot one end of wick and trim knot (this becomes bottom end of the candle).
(c) Cut wick off at top end of candle, leaving approximately 14 cm.

To page 12 ▶

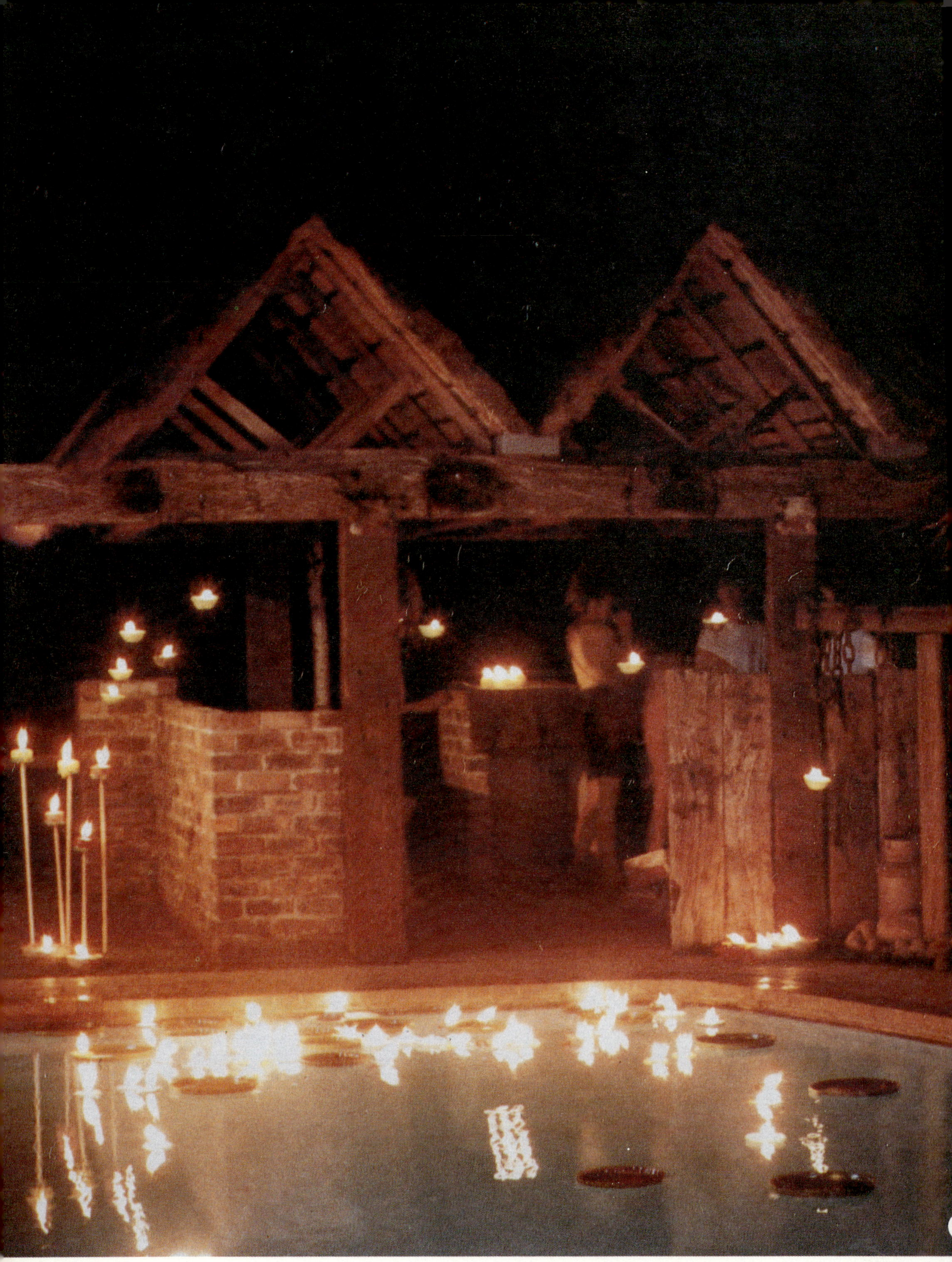

8 *Entertaining out of doors with candles.*

9 *Wax leaves (p. 20), exotic flowers (p. 20), large outdoor floating candles (p. 12) and large wax bowl (p. 17) with perfumed floating candles (p. 9).*

10 *An attractive water feature.*

11 *Garden candles.*

12 *Garden candle comprising a ball candle nestling in a wax bowl top (p. 13).*

11

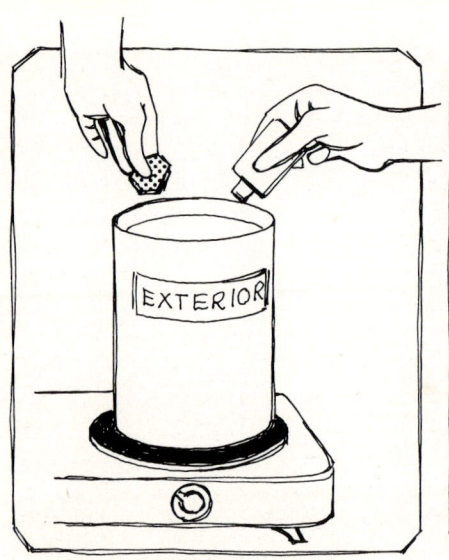

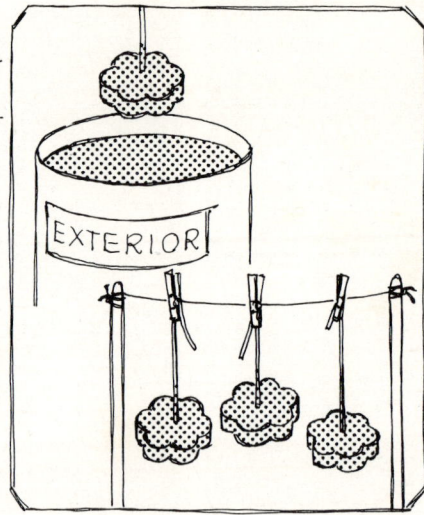

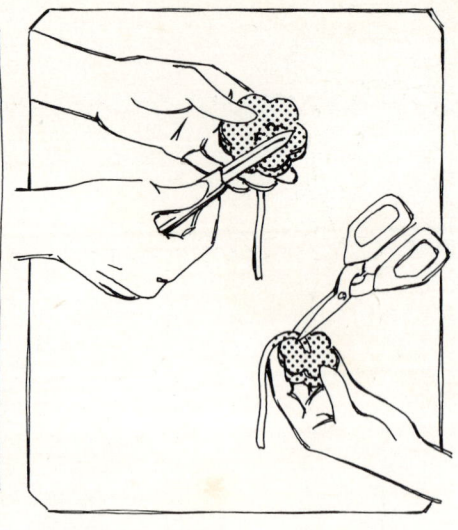

Step 6
(a) When *Exterior* wax reaches 90°C, add colour chip and perfume, and stir until chip has dissolved.
(b) Dip candle into *Exterior* wax and remove quickly.
(c) Hang on 'washing-line' using clothes pegs and dip next candle. Continue in this way until 4 candles have been dipped once. Dip these 4 candles another two times each in the same way.

Step 7
(a) Using a knife cut off wax 'dripping' from bottom of candle while still warm. Rub with finger to smooth and put on flat surface to cool completely, rub with a soft cloth to shine.
(b) Trim wicks to 1 cm each.

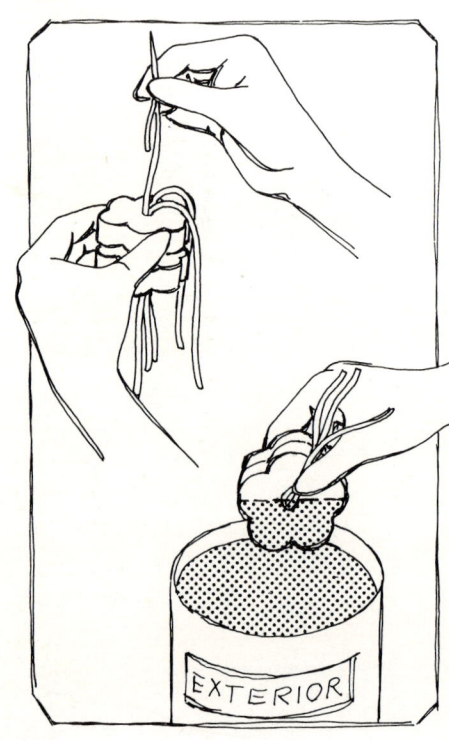

Flower-shaped floating candles

This very attractive floating candle is also perfumed and to make you will need three daisy-shaped cutters ranging from large, medium to small.

To make this candle follow all the *instructions for perfumed floating candles* on page 9 but at *Step 2* do not fill the baking sheet to the brim, only cover the surface of the baking sheet with *Interior* wax.

After you have cut out the wax shapes as in *Step 3*, lift the wax shapes from the baking sheet while still warm and using fingers turn the sides of the shapes upwards. Put the shapes on top of one another, with the smallest on top and the largest at the bottom. Using a sosatie stick pierce a hole through all three shapes and set aside to cool completely.

Continue from *Step 5* to *Step 7*.

Outdoor floating candles

These very beautiful candles may be floated in a large bowl of water on the patio, on ponds and also on the swimming pool. To make an outdoor floating candle use a cutter with a diameter of at least 7 cm. Follow the *instructions for making perfumed floating candles on page 9* but at *Step 5* thread a double instead of a single wick into the candle. This ensures that the breeze will not extinguish the flame.

Large outdoor floating candles

These candles are very suitable for the pool and should burn approximately five hours. A cutter with a diameter of at least 9 cm will be required and to make simply follow *instructions for making perfumed floating candles* on page 9 (although the perfume can be left out). At *Step 5* thread three wicks instead of a single wick into two wax shapes placed on top of each other instead of a single wax shape. In *Step 6* first hold the candle in your hand and dip one side to keep the two shapes in position and then continue dipping as in *Step 6*. Complete as in *Step 7,* but trim wick to 2,5 cm.

Garden candles

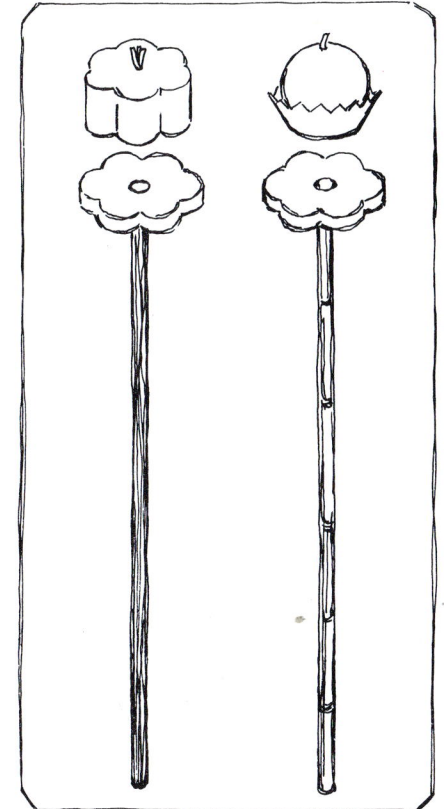

These candles are set upon a dowel or bamboo stick for display amongst plants in the garden.

It is made up of a *stick, base* and *candle* which may be either a *large outdoor floating candle* or a *ball candle nestling in a wax bowl*.

Make the wax shape which forms the base of the garden candle by following the instructions for *perfumed floating candles on page 9* but use a cutter with a diameter of approximately 10 cm. At *Step 4* use the dowel or bamboo stick to make the hole instead of a sosatie stick.

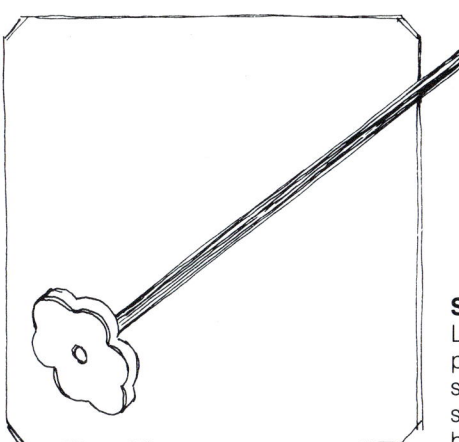

Step 5
Leave shapes in baking sheet to cool completely after which the dowel or bamboo stick is pushed through the hole in the wax shape until it is flush with the top of the base.

Step 6
(a) When *Exterior* wax reaches 90°C add colour chip and stir until dissolved.

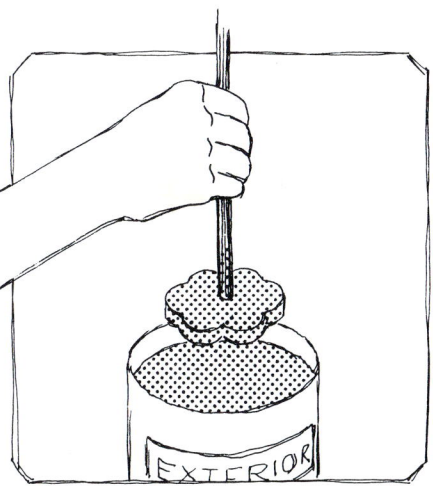

(b) With stick in hand dip the base and approximately 3 cm of the stick into the *Exterior* wax. Wait 60 seconds and repeat. After another 60 seconds repeat dipping once more.

(c) Set aside to cool. (A box filled with sand makes an excellent holder while you are working.)

To page 16 ▶

13 *Hanging wax bowl (p. 17) with perfumed floating candles (p. 9).*

14 *Sand and glue candles (p. 50), exotic flowers (p. 20) and quick and easy sand candles (p. 51).*

15 *Painted sand and glue pebble candles (p. 50).*

15

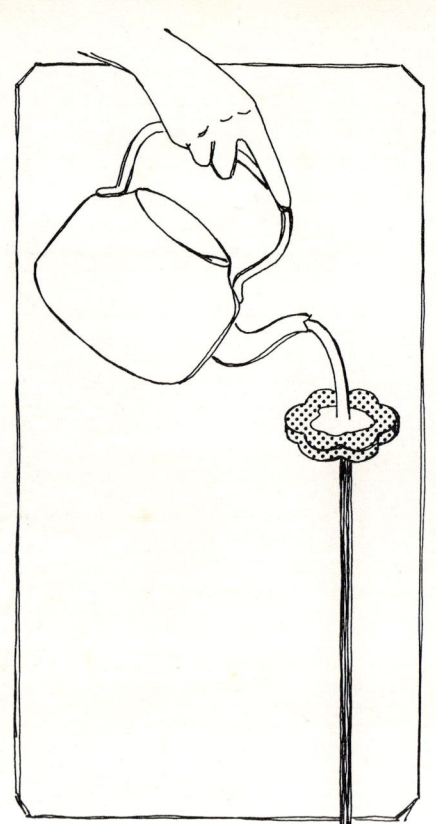

Garden candle with large outdoor floating candle 'top'

If you wish to use the large outdoor floating candle for the top of your garden candle, follow the instructions for large outdoor floating candles on page 12. Join this candle to the base by pouring a little melted wax onto the base and fix the outdoor floating candle onto it. You will have to work very quickly since the candle will not stick properly if the wax has cooled too much.

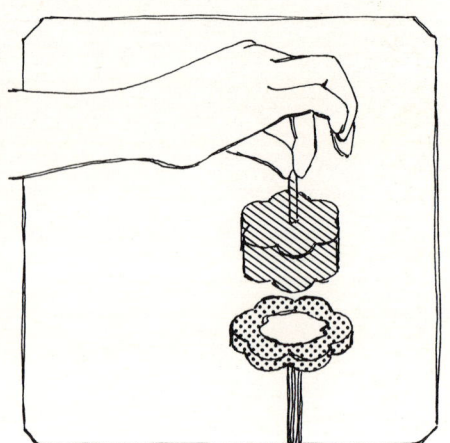

Garden candle with a ball candle nestling in a wax bowl

If you wish to use the ball candle nestling in a wax bowl for the top of your garden candle, you must first make a ball candle as instructed on page 21, remembering to fit it with a triple wick instead of a single wick.

To make the wax bowl follow the instructions on page 17.

To put together, work as follows:

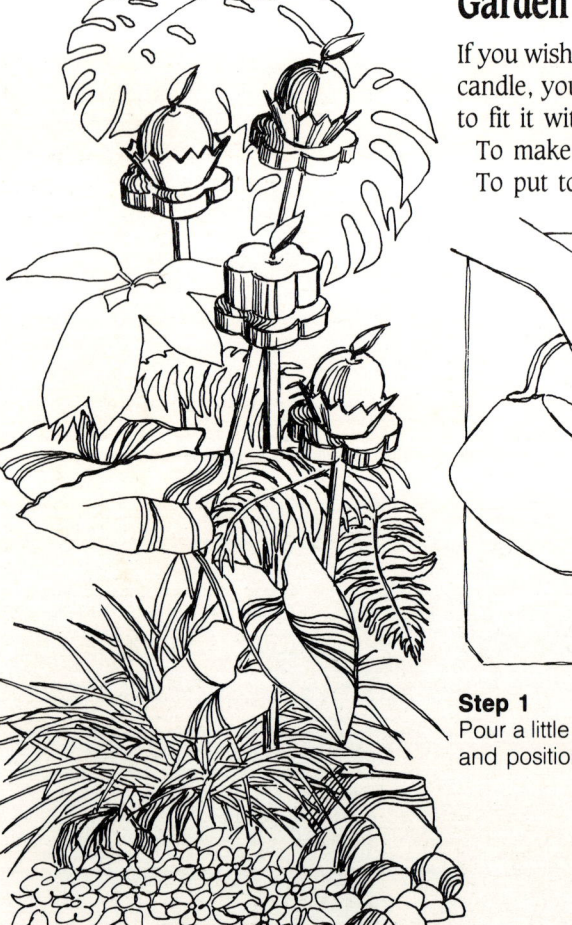

Step 1
Pour a little melted wax into the wax bowl and position the ball candle in the bowl.

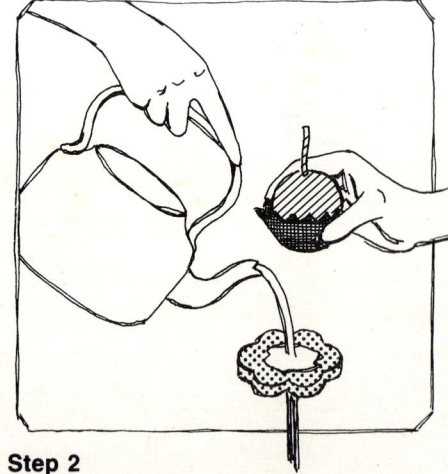

Step 2
Pour a little melted wax onto the base and fix the wax bowl onto it. You must work quickly before the wax sets, or else it will not stick properly.

Important: The garden candle can be made more secure by dipping it once only into *Glossy Sealer* at 103°C.

Wax bowls

These very handy wax bowls are easily made using glass dishes or mixing bowls. When using these wax bowls as hanging bowls, make use of *silicone wire* that cannot catch fire. This wire is available from hardware stores and electrical shops and is usually used in stoves.

Step 1
Melt approx. 100 g *Interior* wax over low heat stirring frequently. When the wax reaches 70°C add a small piece of colour chip and stir.

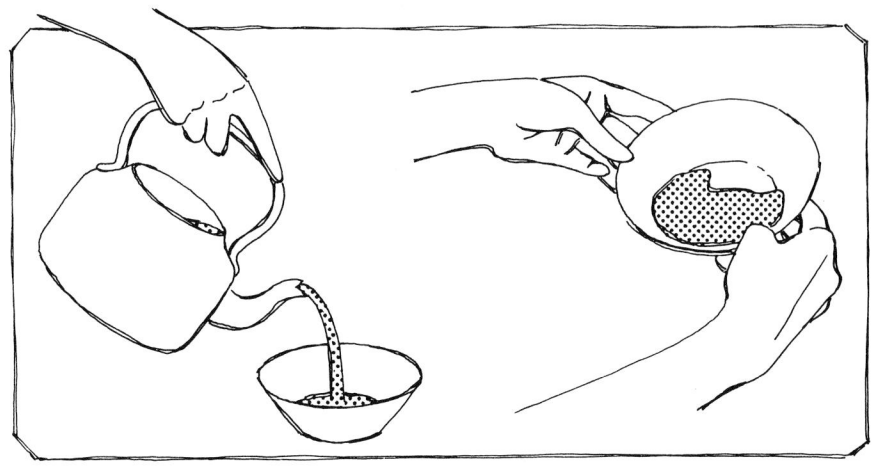

Step 2
(a) Pour a *little* wax into the bowl and
(b) swirl around gently to cover the entire inside of the bowl. Continue swirling until there is no more hot wax left in the bowl. Pour a little wax into the bowl again and swirl. A wax shell is built up in this way on the inside of the bowl.

Step 3
After you have built up this wax shell by pouring and swirling at least 5 times, use a sharp knife and cut a zig-zag or curved design at the top, removing cut-out wax.

Step 4
Immerse this bowl in very cold water and after a few minutes the wax bowl will pop out of the glass bowl.

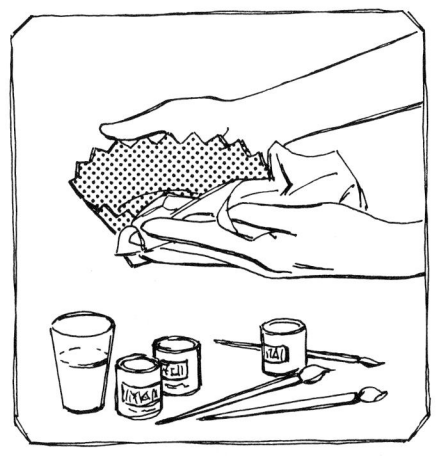

Step 5
Use a paper towel to dry off all water from the wax bowl. At this stage you may paint a design on the wax bowl if you wish. (See p. 46 for decorating candles.)

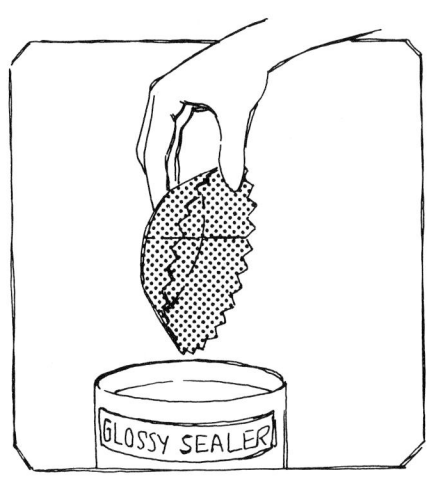

Step 6
Dip your wax bowl, first the one half and then the other into *Glossy Sealer* at 103°C. This will smooth the rough edges where you cut away the border and protect the design if you have painted the candle. Dip once only.

16 *Plump ball candles (p. 21).*

17 *Perfumed floating candles (p. 9) in a pumpkin.*

18 *Sand and glue candles (p. 50).*

19 *A ghostly sight: ghosts (p. 45), spider (p. 41) and pumpkin (p. 40).*

Exotic flower candle

This very versatile candle may be used on its own or floated on the pool either alone or perched on a wax leaf. It may also be used in a display amongst sand candles on the patio.

Step 1
Make a large outdoor floating candle (see p. 12) but do not trim the wick on completion.

Step 2
Make copies of the patterns on p. 52 of this book (nos. 1, 2 and 3) onto sheets of wax paper.

Step 3
Melt 500 g *Interior* wax over low heat stirring frequently until wax reaches 75°C.

Step 4
Divide the melted wax into 3 portions by pouring into two other jugs (containers). Add a different colour to each container, e.g. yellow, orange and red.

Step 5
(a) Pour the darkest colour onto wax sheet 1 at 75°C. Wait for wax to set (about 2 min.).
(b) Using a pair of scissors cut out wax according to the shape of the wax paper and pull away the wax sheet.

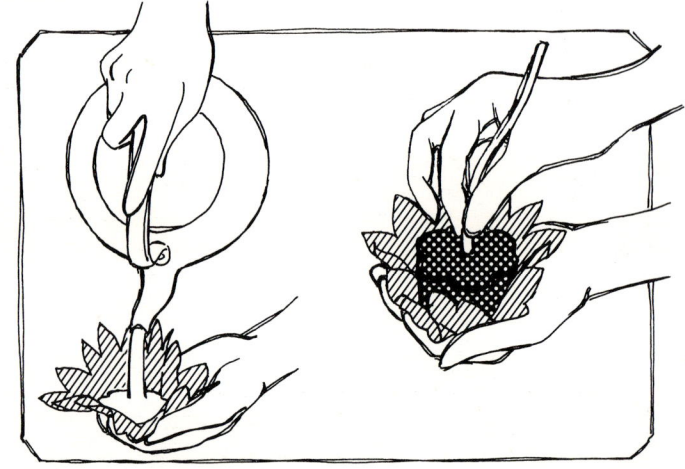

Step 6
(a) Hold the piece of wax you have cut out in your hand and pour a little of the melted wax onto it.
(b) Fold it up around the bottom of the large outdoor floating candle.

Step 7
Using the second darkest colour repeat step 5 onto sheet 2 and fix this second row of petals as in Step 6.

Step 8
Repeat Steps 5 and 6 with the remaining coloured wax poured onto sheet 3.

Step 9
Leave candle to cool completely, then dip into *Glossy Sealer* at 103°C once only. Trim wick to 3 cm.

Wax leaves

These leaves are easy to make and are an attractive feature in the swimming pool.

They are made in the same way as the wax bowls on page 17 but instead of using bowls use a circular tray or large tart dishes. Pour melted wax into the tray or dish and swirl as in *Step (a)* and *(b)* for wax bowls. Repeat this process at least 7 times. It is not necessary, however, to cut a design at the top as in *Step 3*. Instead of immersing this tray or tart dish in cold water you may simply hold it for a while under running cold water. When dipping your 'wax leaf' into *Glossy Sealer* at 103°C as in *Step 6* remember that the leaf will probably be too big for an ordinary dipping pot and therefore it would be a good idea to have the *Glossy Sealer* in a metal basin.

Candles in chocolate moulds

The ball shapes, egg shapes and shell shapes used in this book are but a few of the varieties available. Whatever shape you are using, you will be working with a two-part mould which means that you will make the two halves of the candle separately and will then have to join them.

Before you begin prepare a cardboard box by cutting out a space into which the chocolate mould will fit, so that it hangs suspended.

Step 1
Melt *Interior* wax over low heat in kettle, stirring frequently to distribute heat evenly.

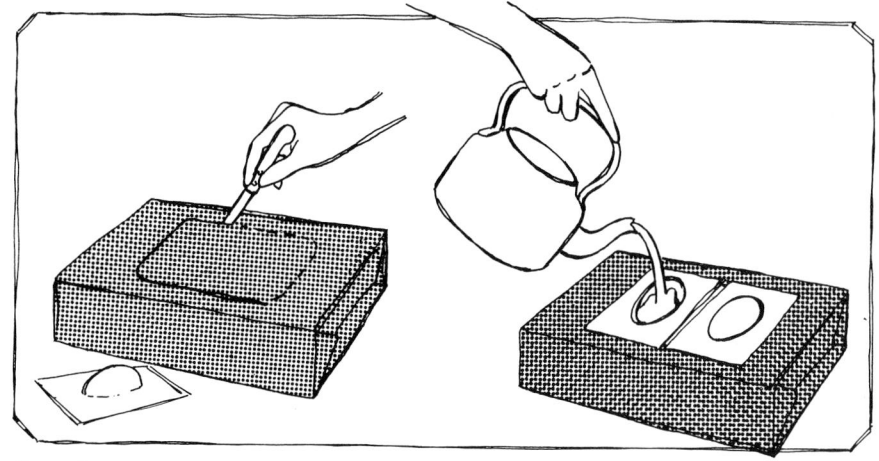

Step 2
Pour *Interior* wax (60°C) into suspended chocolate moulds. Leave to cool completely. The candles will fall out of the moulds easily when cool.

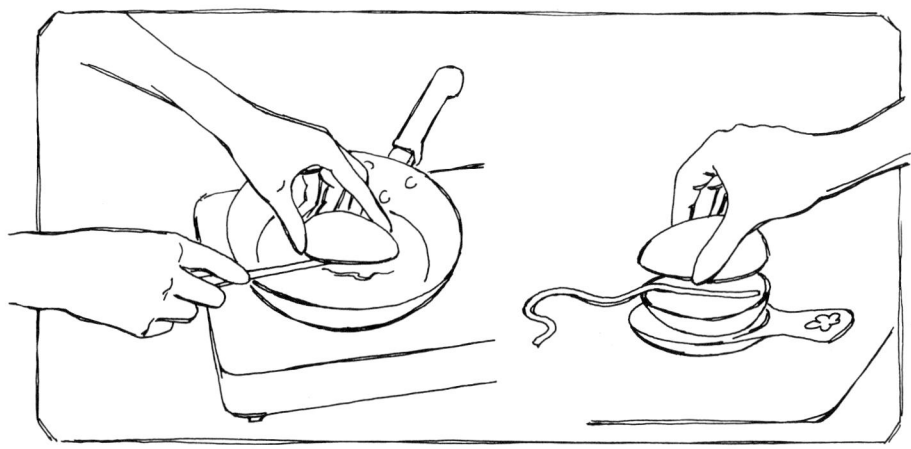

Step 3
(a) In a pan and over very low heat melt the flat side of one half of the candle slightly, flick it into your hand with a knife, and lay it down on a spoon rest.
(b) Place a length of wick across it, and
(c) pour a little of the hot wax from the pan over the wick (wipe outside of pan).

(d) Melt the other half of the candle in the same way and press the two halves tightly together.

Step 4
Should any 'gaps' occur between the two halves, close up using *Interior* wax that has cooled to a gelled state (like cake icing).

To page 24 ▶

20 Entertaining with flowers and candles.

21 For your daughter's birthday: cylindrical (p. 28) and ball candles (p. 21) arranged on a sheet of glass, which in turn is balanced on an overturned decorated champagne glass and held together with Prestik. Wax bowls (p. 17) with flower floating candles (p. 12) round off the display.

22 A plain cylindrical candle (p. 28) in a candle holder made up of two champagne glasses decorated with flowers.

23 Dipped candle set amongst flowers (p. 32).

22

23

23

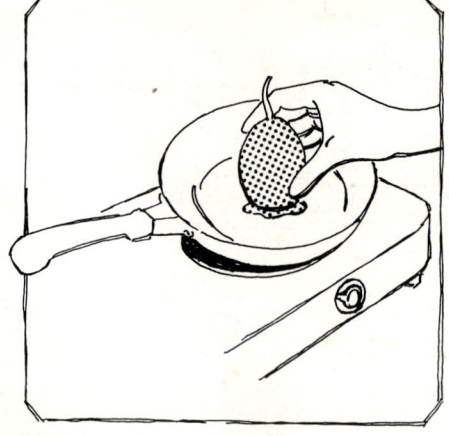

Step 5
Melt *Exterior* wax over low heat until it reaches 90°C. Add perfume and colour chip and stir until dissolved. Dip candle 3 to 5 times allowing 1 minute cooling time before each dipping. Set aside to cool.

Step 6
At this stage your candle is ready for decorating with paint, wax appliqué or pressed flowers (see page 46). Should you want the candle plain, finish off by melting the bottom over low heat until level and trimming the wick to 1 cm. Shine with a soft cloth.

In the same way you can make two half candles in glass bowls and here you may make holes for the wick while the wax is set but still warm.

The two halves are then joined by threading the wick that has previously been dipped into wax through both halves, making a knot at the bottom, and filling the middle with *Interior* wax that has cooled to a gelled state. The candle is then dipped into *Exterior* wax as in *Step 5* and completed as in *Step 6*.

Improvised moulds

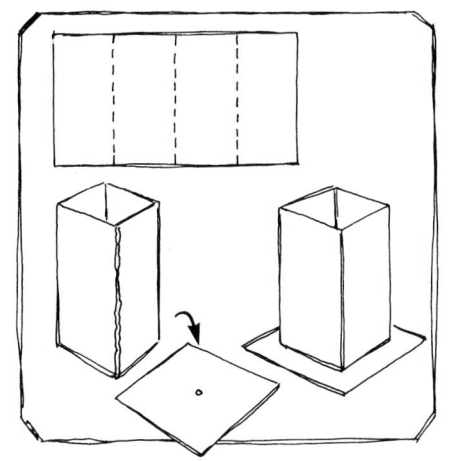

Proper metal candle moulds or alternatively improvised moulds like cans, polish tins, milk cartons, or toilet cardboard rolls may be used to make candles. These moulds are rigid and consist of a non-flexible material, unlike the rubber moulds which can be rolled away from the candle. The following moulds can be made easily from items found around the home.

Cans (vegetable, fish, etc.) – Use a tin opener that cuts from the side and not from the top. Puncture or drill a hole in the centre of the base of the tin.

Polish tin (e.g. a Brasso tin) – Use a tin opener that cuts from the side and cut off the bottom end of the tin. At the top end pierce a hole in the screw-on cap.

Metal medicine containers (e.g. Cal-C-Vita) – Pierce a hole in the base of the container.

Milk cartons – Pierce a hole in the base of the carton.

Cardboard rolls (found in toilet paper, wax wrap, etc.) – Glue roll to a cardboard base that has a hole made in the centre of it. When using these cardboard rolls as moulds it is necessary to wipe the inside of the roll with dishwashing liquid to prevent the wax from penetrating the cardboard. If a very long cardboard roll is used it may be supported by standing it in a container such as a jug.

Large square moulds – Can be made from hard cardboard by cutting a large strip from a cardboard box and folding it into a square. Using wood glue, glue the two open sides together and glue the entire shape onto the square cardboard base into which a hole has been pierced in the centre. Secure these joins on the outside with masking tape. Once again the inner surface must be wiped with dishwashing liquid to prevent wax penetration.

Cone-shaped moulds – Take a square piece of cardboard (not very thick, or else you will not be able to bend it) and roll into a cone shape. Secure joining side with tape. Cut the narrowest end level and glue to a cardboard base into which a hole was made. Cut level the top opening as well. Remember to wipe the inside of this mould with dishwashing liquid to prevent wax penetration. If this mould is very tall you may stand it in a container, e.g. a jug, to obtain support.

N.B. *Do not use aerosol containers since it is dangerous to pierce such cans.*

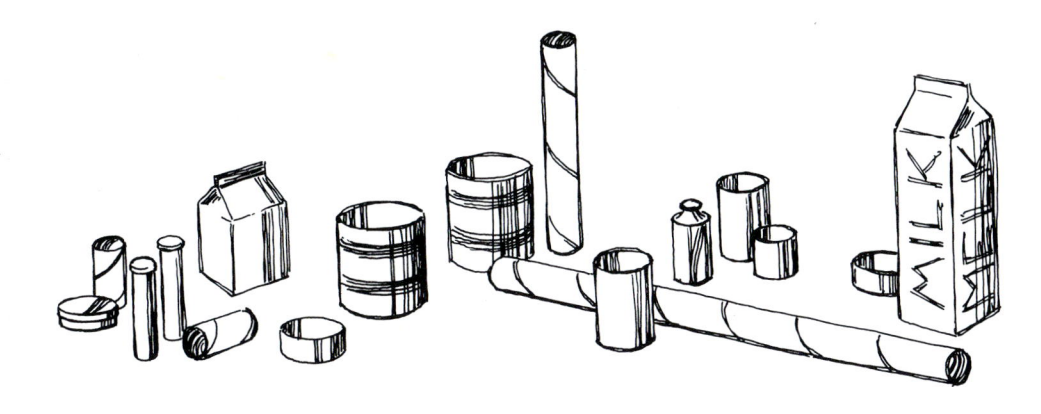

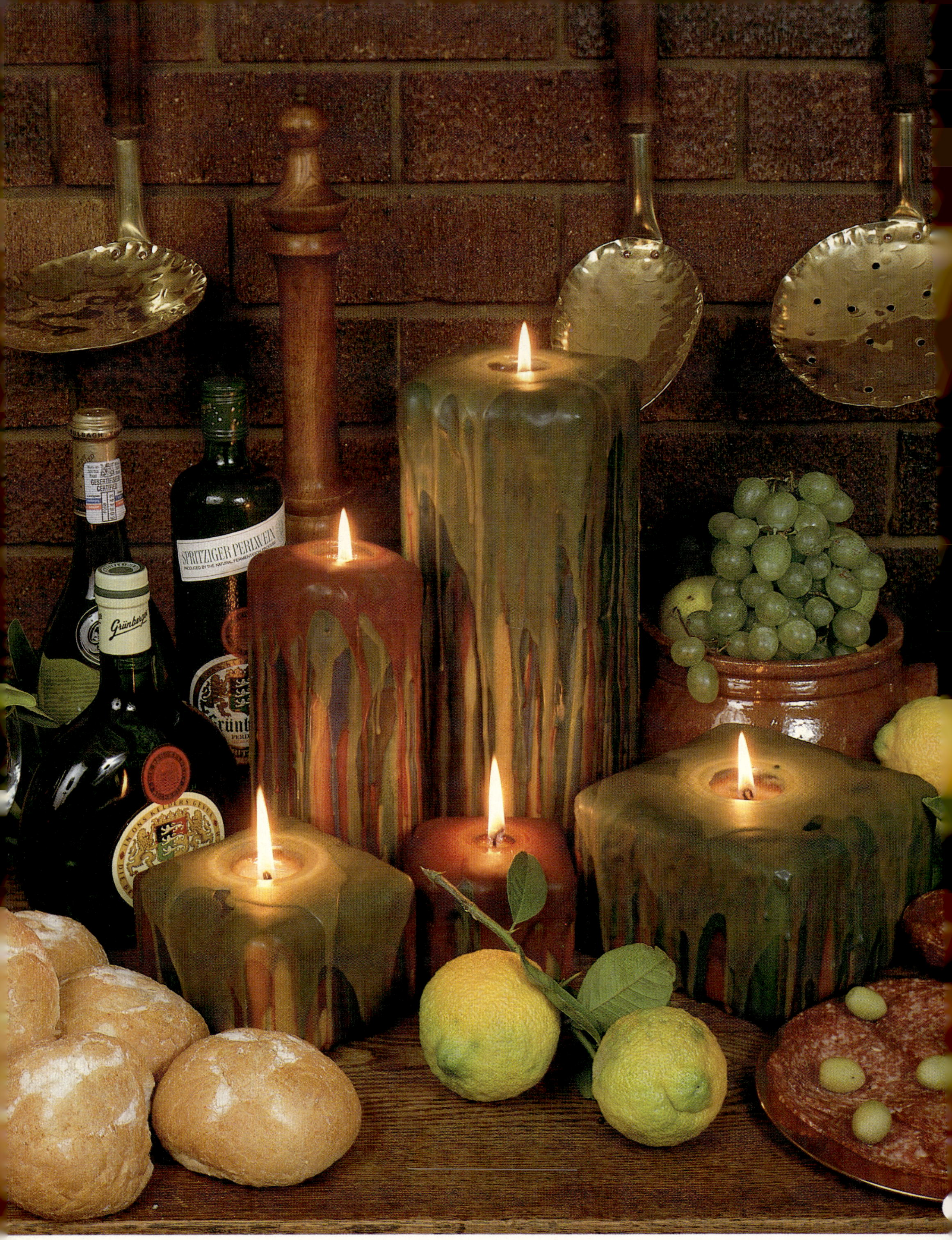
SPRITZIGER PERLWEIN
Grünberger

24 Large square candles (p. 29) made in improvised cardboard moulds (p. 25), create a cosy atmosphere.

25 Old country charm: The cone-shaped and cylindrical candles were made in improvised cardboard moulds (p. 25), the square candles in milk cartons (instructions for candles on page 28) and the ball candles in chocolate moulds (p. 21).

Candles made using improvised moulds

The instructions below are not intended for very large improvised cardboard moulds and the instructions for large candles on page 29 should be followed if you are using such a mould. If you are using a can, tin or milk carton you may proceed as follows:

Step 1

Place *Interior* wax in kettle and heat over very low heat. Put *Exterior* wax into dipping pot and after step 3 you may start melting it over low heat.

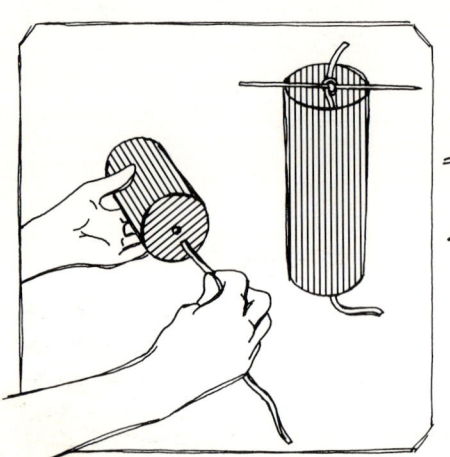

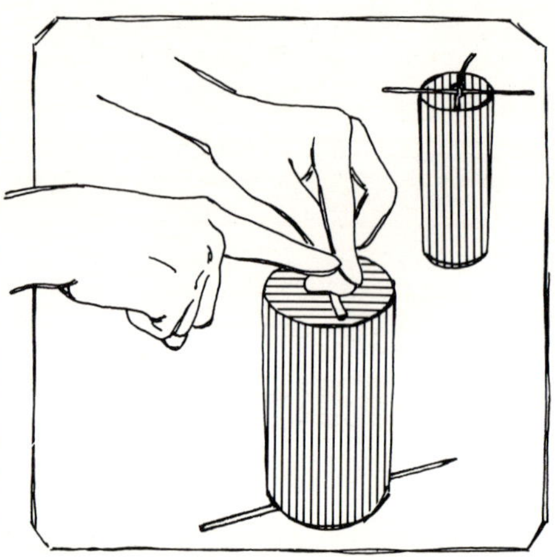

Step 2
(a) Thread mould (tin) by inserting a length of wick that has been dipped in melted wax through the small hole in the bottom of the mould.
(b) At the top open end of the mould use a piece of sosatie stick and tie wick securely to it.
(c) At the bottom end of the mould pull wick tight and secure with Prestik.
(d) The mould is now ready for casting.

Step 3

When *Interior* wax reaches 60°C, pour into mould and allow to cool. After approx. 45 minutes, wax would have cooled but filling would be required. Use *Interior* wax at 90°C for filling up. Leave to cool completely.

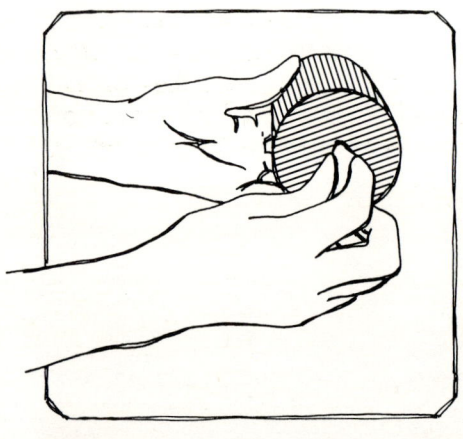

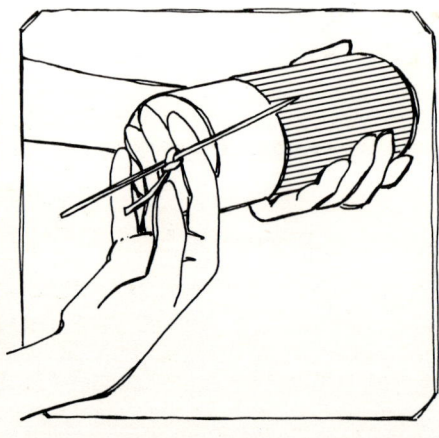

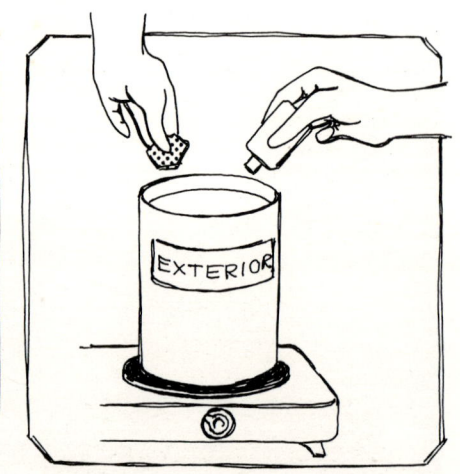

Step 4

When candle has cooled, remove Prestik from bottom of mould, grasp sosatie stick and pull candle from mould. (N.B. If difficult to remove, place mould in freezer for 15 minutes.) If you have used a cardboard mould, you might have to tear it off. Remove sosatie stick and cut off wick on bottom end of candle.

Step 5
(a) When *Exterior* wax reaches 90°C, add colour chip and perfume and stir until dissolved.

(b) Hold candle by the wick, dip into *Exterior* wax and remove quickly. Hold candle above dipping pot for 60 seconds. Repeat this dipping process another three times. Let candle cool completely.

Step 6
Heat an old pan over low heat, hold candle firmly and melt bottom of candle until it stands level.
At this stage the candle is ready for appliqué work, decorative painting or the addition of pressed flowers if so desired. See section on decorating, page 46.

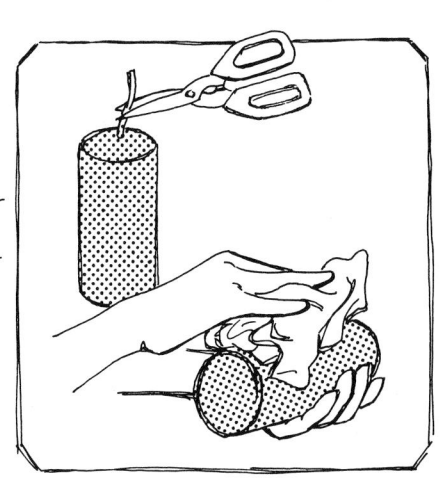

Step 7
Trim wick to 1 cm and rub candle with a clean cloth to 'shine'.

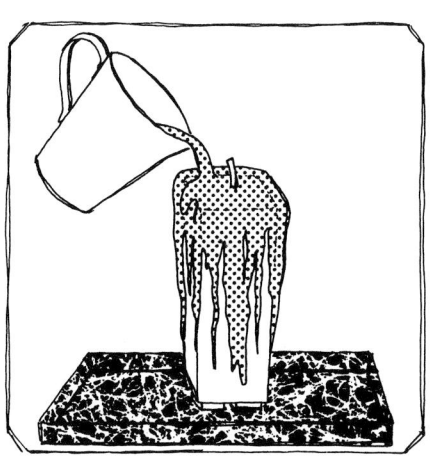

Large candles made in improvised moulds

As previously stated (see p. 25) moulds can be made from cardboard in square, cylindrical, pyramid, cone shapes, etc. However, when making very large candles, too much melted wax on the inside of the mould can cause the mould to leak.

Therefore follow instructions for candles made using improvised moulds on page 28 but at *Step 3* pour only a little wax into the mould and scatter a layer of *Interior* wax cubes (unmelted) over it. Pour a layer of melted *Interior* wax (60°C) over these cubes and scatter wax cubes again. Continue in this way until you have filled the mould with wax. Leave to cool completely and follow *Steps 4, 5, 6 and 7*. However, if the candle is too large to be dipped completely into the *Exterior* wax, hold the candle firmly and dip first the bottom end and then the top end. Allow 60 seconds cooling time before each dipping. Repeat this process until the entire candle has been dipped three times.

If the candle to be dipped into the *Exterior* wax is too heavy you may obtain an interesting finish by pouring different colours of melted *Exterior* wax over the candle (see p. 26) instead of dipping it. This is done by standing the candle on a baking sheet with an object placed under the candle so that there is a gap between candle and baking sheet where excess wax can flow (which can be retrieved for later use).

30

26 *A group of owls (p. 36).*

27 *Blue birds of happiness (p. 44).*

28 *Candles for interior decorating: hand moulded mushrooms (p. 44) and tomatoes (p. 36).*

29 *A group of Russian dolls which brighten up the coffee table (p. 36).*

Dipped candles

These very useful candles can be made as thick, thin, tall or short as you want. Colour them as desired and perfume them to make them really special.

Step 1
Melt *Exterior* wax in a very tall dipping pot. When wax has melted add colour chip and perfume and stir until dissolved.

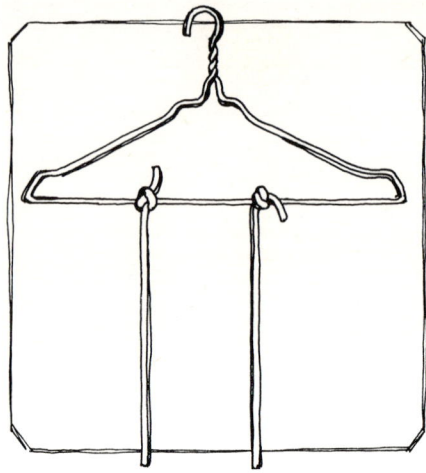

Step 2
Tie 2 pieces of wick to a coat-hanger. Remember that the wick should not be longer than the dipping pot.

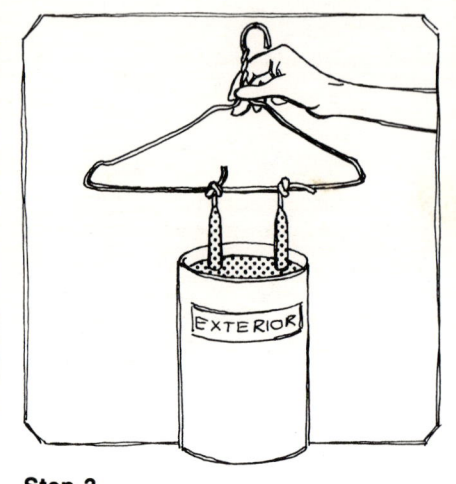

Step 3
When *Exterior* wax has reached 90°C dip the wicks once and hang up to cool for 2 minutes. Continue the dipping and cooling process until your candle is the required thickness.

Because you have to wait 2 minutes after each dipping, your time can be used more effectively if you work with 10 coat-hangers (20 candles) at a time.

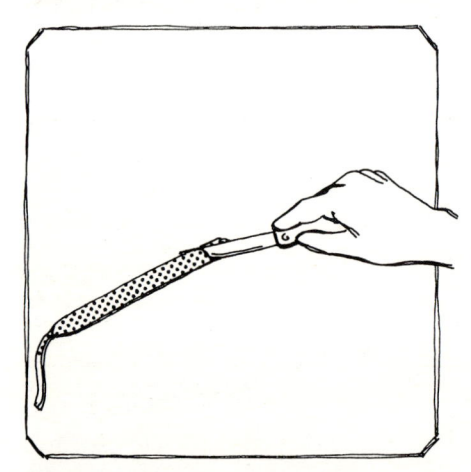

Step 4
On completion of a dipped candle and while it is still warm, cut it level at the bottom with a knife. When completely cool trim wick at the top of the candle to 1 cm and shine with a soft cloth.

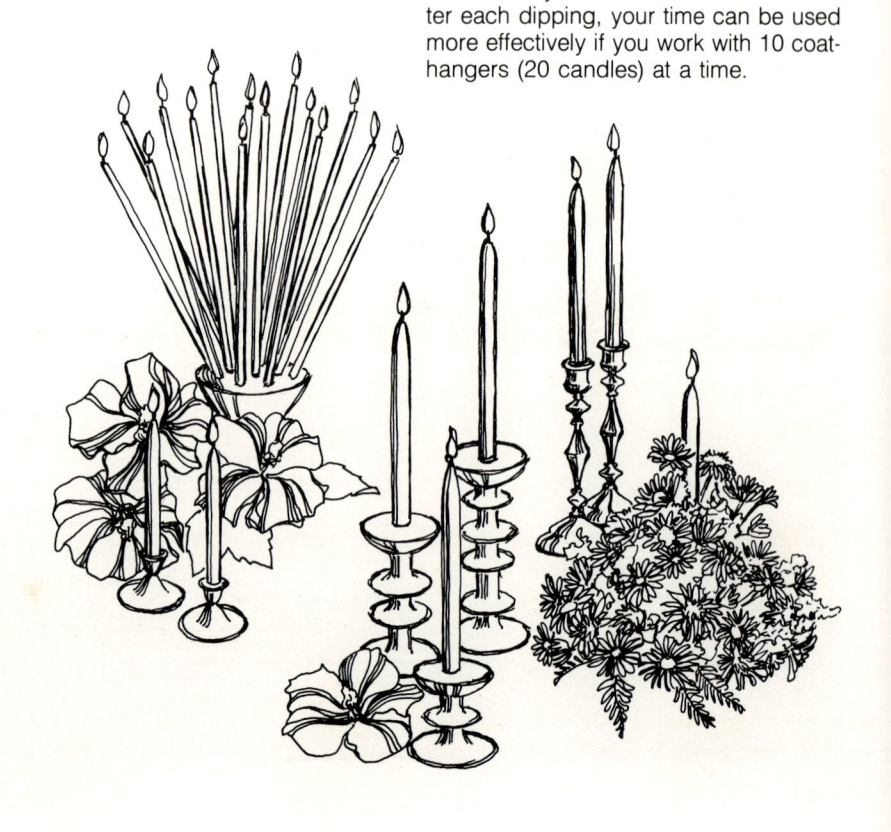

Hand-moulded candles

This is one of the most exciting candle-making techniques. The creative possibilities are endless (see pp. 30, 31, 38, 39) and because no moulds are required it is greatly favoured by children whose co-ordination and creativity are stimulated at the same time.

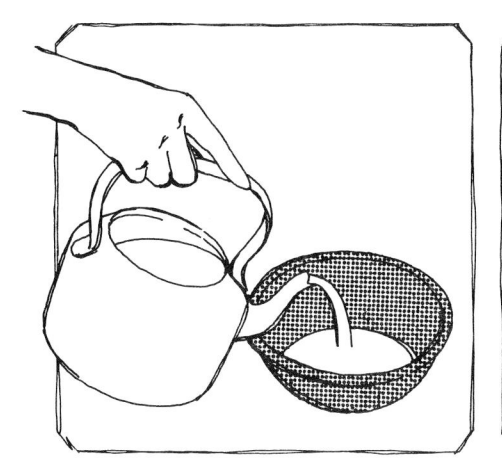

Step 1
After placing *Interior* wax in kettle, heat over low heat and stir frequently to distribute heat evenly. When wax reaches 60°C, pour into a mixing bowl and stir wax gently until it is cool enough to handle.

Step 2
Put *Exterior* wax in dipping pot and melt over low heat.

Step 3
Take a small amount of cooled *Interior* wax into your hand and press into shape. Leave to cool. Ignore cracks in the candle as they will be covered when dipped into *Exterior* wax.

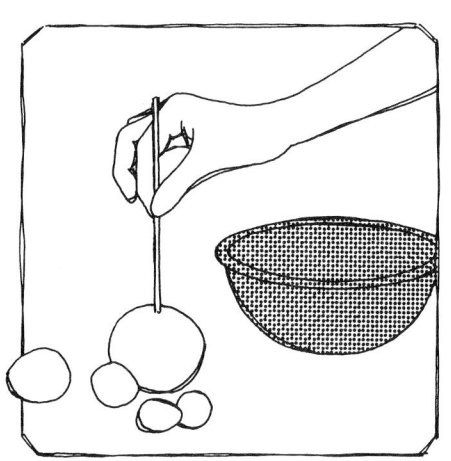

Step 4
When candle is set but still warm, pierce a hole through the middle using a sosatie stick. Leave to cool completely.

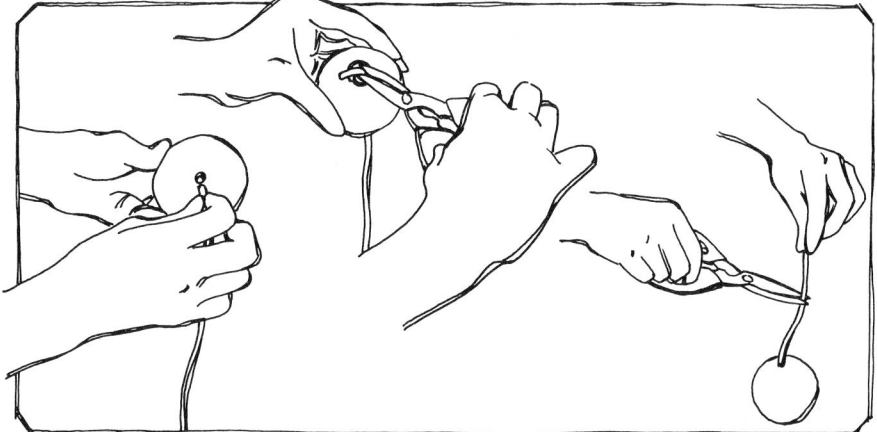

Step 5
(a) Thread wick which has been dipped in wax through the hole in the candle and knot wick at bottom end. (The knot must be big and secure or else your candle may fall into the dipping pot.)
(b) Trim knot.
(c) The wick at the top of the candle should be approximately 7 cm long.

To page 36 ▶

30 Candles for Christmas: large ball candle with wax applique (p. 21), small painted ball candles, (p. 21) and cone-shaped candles made in metal pastry horns (p. 49). The wreath was made of willow laths secured with satin ribbons.

31 These candles have proved to be the most popular fête or gift items. On top of the shelf: a hand painted Russian doll (p. 36), a packet of ball candles (p. 21) and a plain cylindrical candle (p. 28). Below the shelf: a basket of perfumed floating candles which may be sold individually out of the basket at the fête; perfumed floating candles (p. 9), packed in linen bags (can also be used as potpourri for the linen cupboard); plain cylindrical candle; a ball candle decorated with pressed flowers (p. 21); a tulle bag with dipped candles (p. 32); and a painted wax bowl (p. 17) with perfumed floating candles.

32 Long dipped candles (p. 32) in a sand and glue container (p. 51).

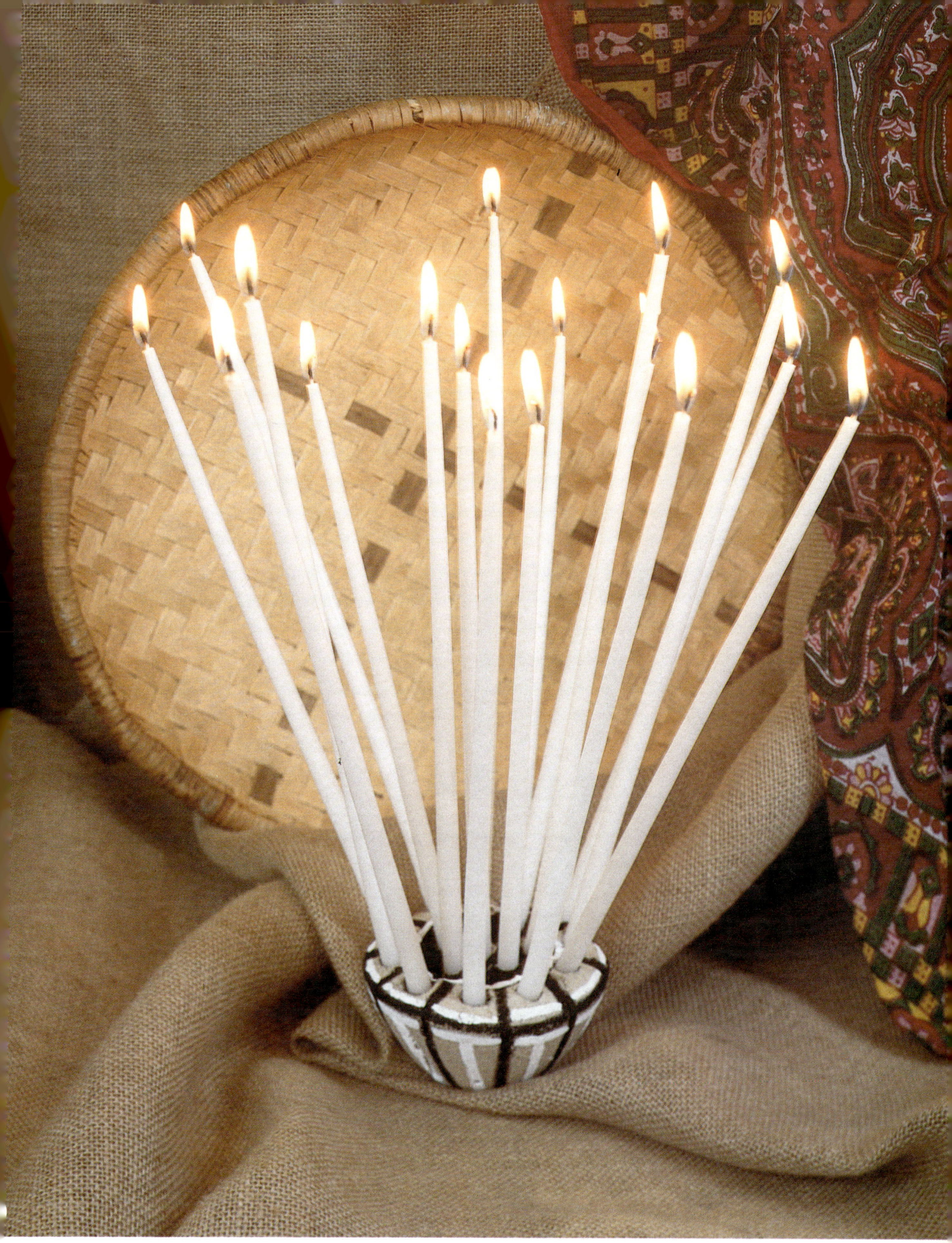

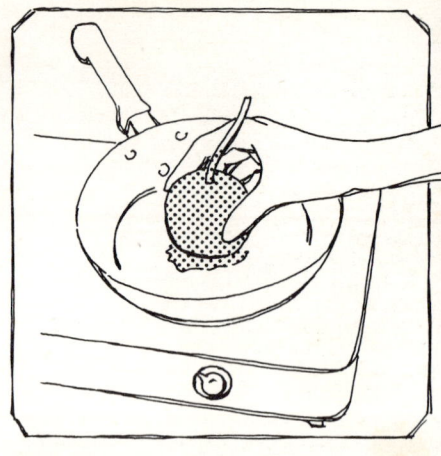

Step 6

(a) When *Exterior* wax reaches 90°C add colour chip and stir until dissolved.

(b) Dip the candle gently but quickly into *Exterior* wax and hold away from dipping pot while waiting for candle to cool (2 min.). Repeat dipping process another 3 times. (Candle should be dipped at least 4 times.) Allow candle to cool completely.

Step 7

Heat old pan over low heat, hold candle and melt until level. (Only if candle needs to be levelled.) When candle has cooled completely, trim wick to 1 cm and rub candle with soft cloth to 'shine'. However, should you wish to decorate your candle (see section on decorating, p. 46) this should be done after melting the candle level but before trimming the wick.

Hand-moulded beetle

Follow all the instructions for a hand-moulded candle on page 33 but instead of moulding a ball shape, make a flatter oblong shape (beetle shape). On completion do not trim wick but paint the candle first as instructed on page 46.

Tomato candles

Follow instructions for a hand-moulded candle (p. 33) and on completion do not trim wick but apply the wax leaves according to the wax appliqué method on page 46.

Russian doll candles

Follow instructions for hand-moulded candles (p. 33) but instead of moulding a ball shape, squeeze slightly at the top to give the required pear shape. On completion do not trim wick, but paint the candle first (see instructions on p. 46).

Owls

Follow the instructions for hand-moulded candles (p. 33) but instead of moulding a ball shape, make an oblong shape and make two indentations by means of a gentle pinch at the top to form the eye sockets of the owl. On completion do not trim wick, but paint the candle first. (See instructions on p. 46.)

Wonderworm candle

Follow instructions for hand-moulded candles (p. 33) but at *Step 2* melt the *Exterior* wax in a metal basin rather than in a dipping pot and proceed as follows:

Step 3
Take a small amount of cooled *Interior* wax into your hand and press into ball shapes, pushing the balls together. Leave to cool and ignore small cracks in the candle, which will be covered when dipped into *Exterior* wax later on.

Step 4
When candle is set but still warm pierce a hole through the middle of each ball (segment of worm) using a sosatie stick. Any large cracks in the candle may at this stage be filled with *Interior* wax which has cooled to a gelled state (similar to cake icing).

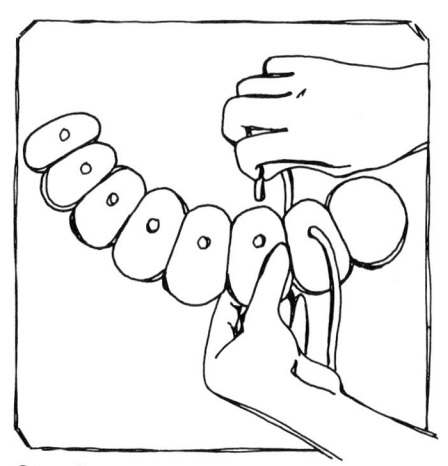

Step 5
(a) When candle has cooled completely, thread wick which has previously been dipped in wax, through each ball and knot wick at bottom end.

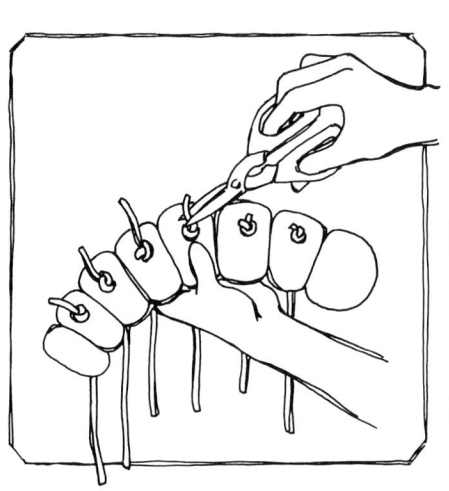

(b) Trim knots.

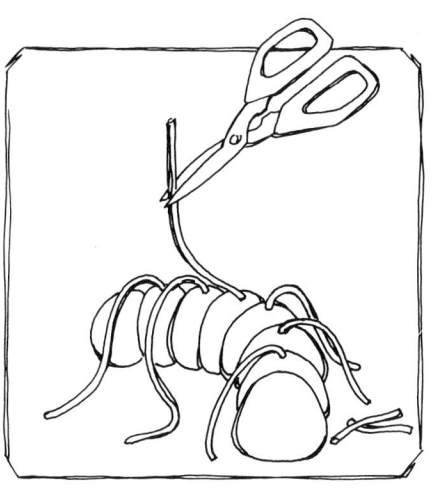

(c) The wicks at the top of the candle should be approx. 17 cm long.

Important

While threading this 'worm' the segments (balls) may loosen from one another. Simply dip the sides of each ball into melted *Interior* wax (60°C) and push them together again.

Step 6
(a) When *Exterior* wax reaches 90°C add colour chip and stir well until chip has melted.

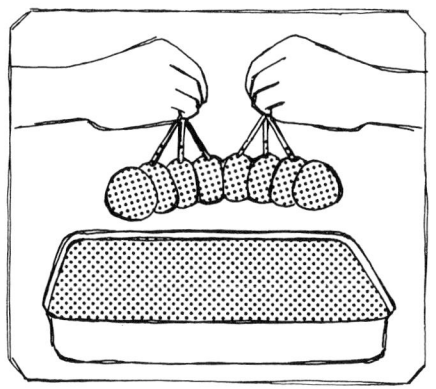

(b) Holding the 'worm' by all the wicks, dip gently but quickly into *Exterior* wax and hold away from dipping pot while waiting for the candle to cool (2 min.).

Repeat dipping process another 3 times. (Candle should be dipped at least 4 times.) Allow candle to cool completely.

At this stage the candle is ready for decoration if desired and may be either painted or decorated with wax appliqué. (See p. 46). After decoration the wicks should be trimmed to 1 cm.

37

33

38

33 *Candles made by children using jelly moulds.*

34 *Cute Cat (p. 44).*

35 *Prison Panther (p. 44).*

36 *Handmoulded garden friends all coming to the party ... Sprightly Spider (p. 41), Billy and Babette beetle (p. 36), Wonderworm (p. 36), and Supersnail (p. 41). Dipped candles in the cake light the way (p. 32).*

Pumpkin

Follow the instructions for hand-moulded candles on page 33, up to and including *Step 3*, but make five balls and place them in a circle on a sheet of wax paper, pushing them from the sides, inwards towards each other.

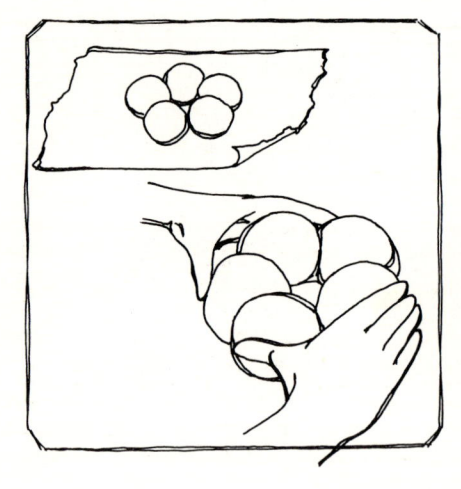

Step 4

(a) Push some *Interior* wax into the middle opening of the 'pumpkin' and lift sheet of wax wrap with the pumpkin on it and place into a flat bowl of a slightly smaller diameter than that of the pumpkin. (This will lift the sides of the pumpkin to make it look more realistic.)

(b) When set but still warm, use a sosatie stick and make a hole in the middle of the pumpkin. Leave to cool completely.

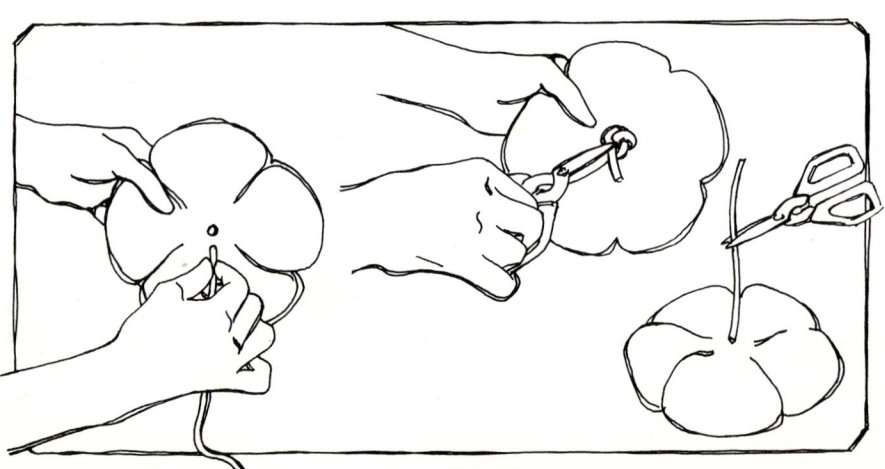

Step 5

Thread wick that has been dipped into wax and make a big knot at the bottom of the candle. (Remember the substantial weight of the candle must be held by this knot.) The wick at the top of the candle should be 10 cm.

N.B.

Should the segments of the pumpkin fall apart while you are working, simply dip the detached parts into hot *Interior* wax (60°C) and stick them together again.

Step 6

When *Exterior* wax reaches 90°C add colour chip and stir until dissolved. Dip candle gently but quickly into *Exterior* wax and hold away from dipping pot while waiting for candle to cool (2 min.). Repeat dipping process another 3 times. (Candle should be dipped at least 4 times.) Allow candle to cool completely.

Step 7

At this stage the candle should be painted (crevices highlighted) (see p. 46). If you wish to leave the pumpkin unpainted, simply trim wick to 1 cm and shine with a soft cloth.

Spider

Follow instructions for hand-moulded candles on page 33 from *Step 1* up to and including *Step 3*, but make two balls, one more than twice the size of the other. Flatten these balls slightly and make four holes with a sosatie stick on each side of the large ball (to fit the legs) as well as a hole from the top, to allow for the wick.

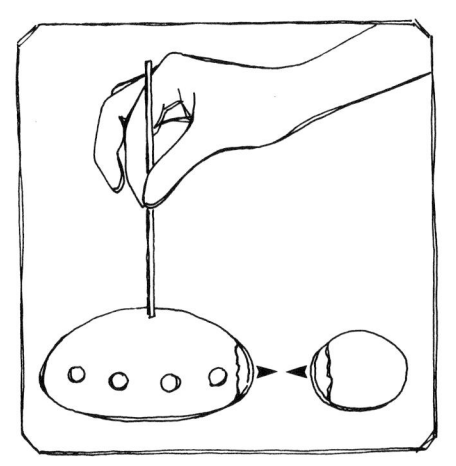

Step 4
Join these 2 balls together by dipping the areas where they are to be joined into melted *Interior* wax (60°C). Quickly push the two balls together. Allow to cool. Thread wick through large ball. (See *Step 5(a), (b), (c)* on p. 33.)

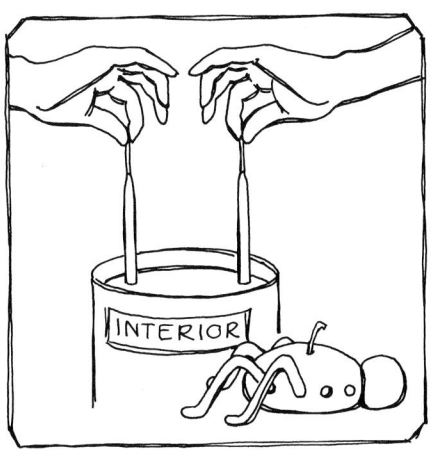

Step 5
Cut 8 lengths of wick approx. 12 cm long and dip 2 at a time into melted *Interior* wax (60°C) until they are the required thickness (allow 2 min. cooling time between dips). Allow these 'legs' to cool but while still warm and pliable, dip only the tip of the leg into melted *Interior* wax and fit into the hole you have made in the large ball. Bend the leg into shape and repeat for all 8 legs. Allow candle to cool completely.

Step 6
When *Exterior* wax reaches 90°C add colour chip and stir until dissolved. Dip the 'spider' quickly into *Exterior* wax and hold away from dipping pot while waiting for candle to cool (2 min.). Repeat dipping process once more only and set aside to cool. You may have to bend the legs back into position.

Step 7
Allow candle to cool completely before painting (see p. 46 for decorating instructions) but should you wish to leave the candle unpainted, simply trim the wick to 1 cm and shine candle with a soft cloth.

Snail

Follow instructions for hand-moulded candles on page 33 from *Step 1* up to and including *Step 3* but hand-mould the shell of the snail and the body separately. Stick two pieces of toothpick into the head to represent the horns. Put the shell and body together by dipping the parts to be joined in melted *Interior* wax (60°C) and quickly push them together. Follow *Steps 4, 5, 6* and *7* of the instructions for hand-moulded candles.

37

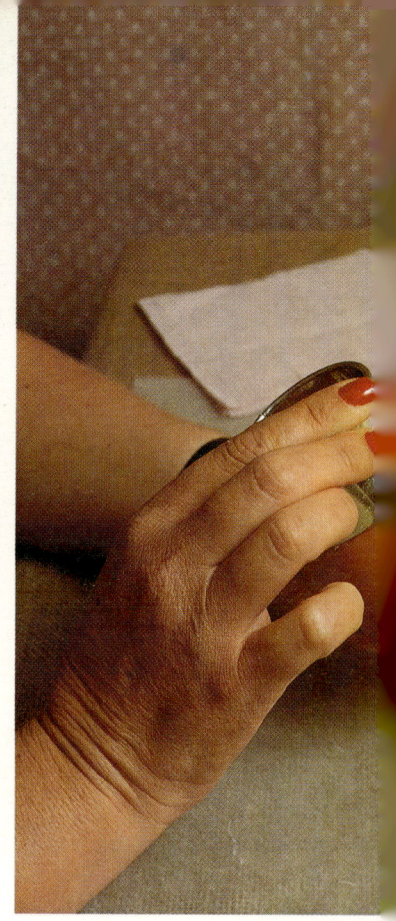

42

37 *Painting candles (p. 46).*

38 *Cutting shapes into a candle with a cutter (p. 47).*

39 *Cutting out shapes with a knife. (p. 47).*

40 *Applying pressed flowers (p. 47).*

41 *Wax appliqué (p. 46).*

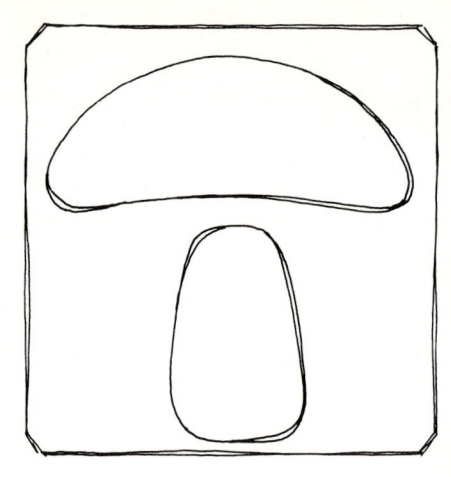

Mushroom

Follow instructions for hand-moulded candles on page 33 from *Step 1* up to and including *Step 3* but make a round flat shape and an oblong shape. Join the two shapes together by dipping the areas to be joined in a little melted *Interior* wax (60°C) and quickly push them together. Follow *Steps 4, 5, 6* and *7* on page 33.

Panther

Follow instructions for hand-moulded candles on page 33 from *Step 1* up to and including *Step 3* but instead of ball shapes, mould the body, head, nose and ears separately. The legs and arms are made in the same way as for the spider (see *Step 5*, p. 41) and remember to make holes in the body into which the arms and legs will fit. The feet are also moulded separately. Put all the pieces together by dipping them into *Interior* wax (60°C) and assemble them quickly. First put the head and body together before joining the limbs. Follow *Steps 4,5,6* and *7* on page 33.

Cat

Follow instructions for hand-moulded candles on page 33 from *Step 1* up to and including *Step 3*, but instead of ball shapes mould the body, limbs, head, ears, nose and eyeballs separately. Dip each separate piece into melted *Interior* wax (60°C) and fix into position, working first with the components of the head and then joining the head to the body. Join limbs to body in the same way. Follow *Steps 4,5,6* and *7* on page 33.

Bird

Follow instructions for hand-moulded candles on page 33 from *Step 1* up to and including *Step 3*, but instead of a ball, mould a longer shape lifting and pinching the one end to form the tail. Mould the head and beak separately. Dip each piece consecutively into melted *Interior* wax (60°C) and assemble them quickly. Follow *Steps 4,5,6* and *7* on page 33.

Ghosts

Follow instructions for hand-moulded candles on page 33 from *Step 1* up to and including *Step 4* but instead of a ball, mould an oblong shape of approx. 8 cm long and 4 cm in diameter. Continue with *Step 5* below before candle has cooled completely.

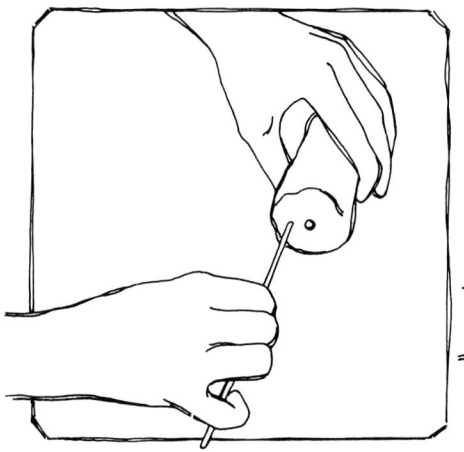

Step 5
Insert a sosatie stick, slightly off centre, approx. 3 cm into the wax at the bottom of the oblong shape. Make sure that the wick hole is still open. Leave to cool completely.

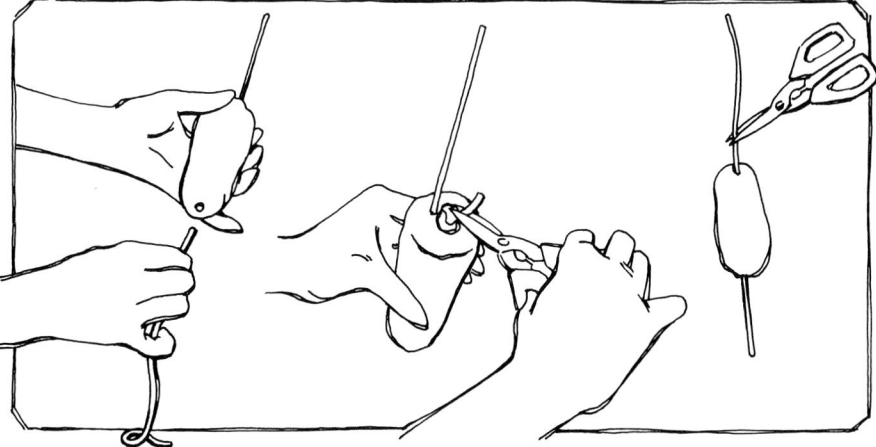

Step 6
(a) Thread wick which has been dipped in wax, through candle and knot at bottom end.
(b) Trim knot.
(c) The wick at the top should be 3 cm long.

Step 7
When *Exterior* wax reaches 90°C, dip the candle holding it by the stick. Allow 1 minute cooling time and repeat this dipping and cooling process another two times making sure that at least 2 cm of the sosatie stick is covered by the wax. This will strengthen the joint.

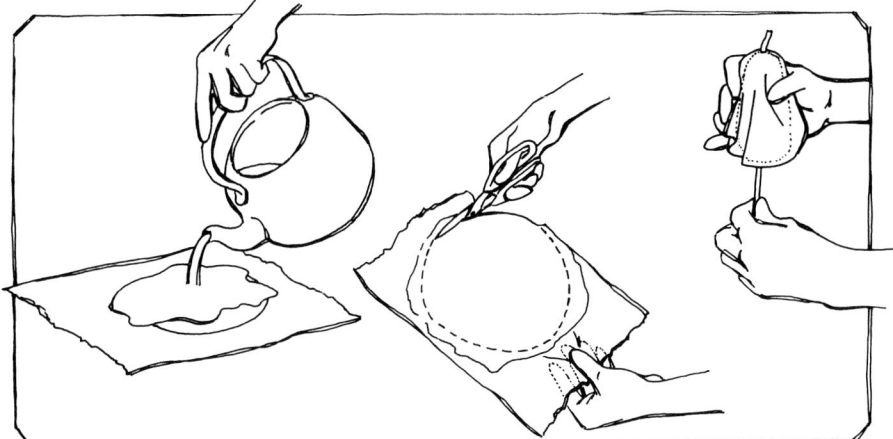

Step 8
(a) Draw a circle with a diameter of approx. 20 cm on a sheet of wax paper. Pour melted *Interior* wax (75°C) on the paper. Allow to set (approx. 2 min.) and (b) cut out with a pair of scissors. Discard the wax wrap and prick a hole in the middle of this piece of wax (with a sosatie stick).
(c) Slide this wax sheet over the candle you have made and fold sides flat. Set aside to cool.

Step 9
Paint eyes as instructed on page 46.

Decorating candles

Although there are many ways in which a candle can be decorated, the most effective methods are painting, wax appliqué and pressed flowers. See photos on page 42 and 43.

Painting

Use poster paints, readily available from stationery shops, for painting on candles. Remember that you can mix your own colours, so you need buy only the basic colours (black, white, red, blue and yellow). Paint on candles in the same way as you would on paper. Leave the painted candles to dry properly and follow the instructions at the end of this section for completing a decorated candle (p. 47).

Wax appliqué

Before appliqué work can be started, a collection of wax shapes in various colours must be made (you can use scraps of *Exterior* wax) as follows:

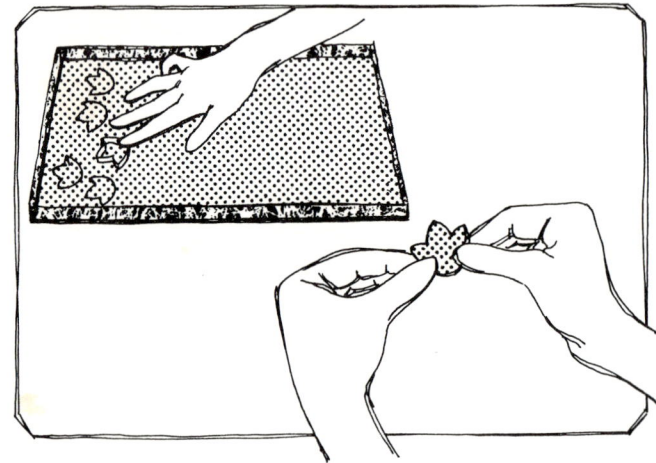

(a) Heat *Exterior* wax over low heat. Add colour.
(b) Pour into baking sheet, only covering the surface of the sheet.
(c) When wax is set but still warm cut out shapes using icing or aspic cutters.

(d) Remove these shapes and mould them into the required shape with your hands, or simply leave them in the baking sheet to cool and apply them as they are to the candle.

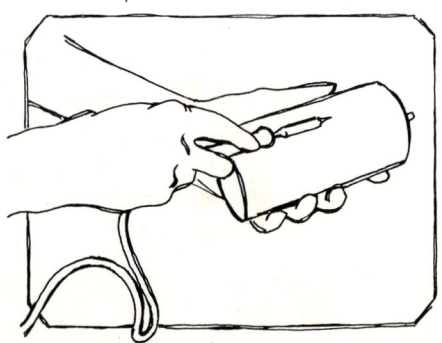

Apply wax shapes to candle as follows:

(a) Heat a small patch on the candle with a soldering iron (25 W).

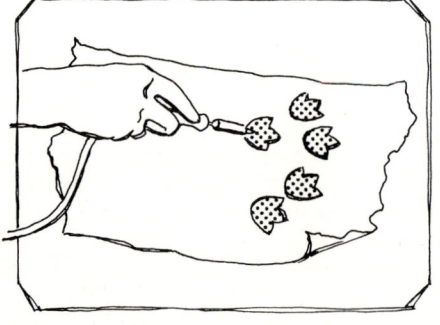

(b) Heat a small patch on the wax shape.

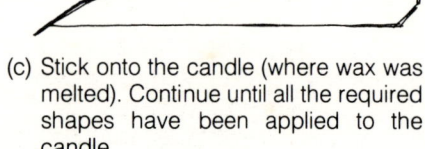

(c) Stick onto the candle (where wax was melted). Continue until all the required shapes have been applied to the candle.

Follow instructions for completing decorated candles on page 47.

Pressed flowers

Press small flowers between two sheets of tissue paper placed in a book such as an old telephone directory. They should be ready for use after three weeks and flowers such as geraniums, alyssum, gypsophila, pansies, etc. press very well. Simply apply paper glue (clear liquid glue) to the dried flowers using a paint brush, and stick the flowers to the candle. Make sure that all the edges are well stuck down, even if you have to paint over the flower with the glue.

Leave to dry thoroughly and follow instructions below for completing decorated candles.

Cutting shapes into a candle

This is not only a very effective way of decorating, but adds an extra dimension in that the cut-away area glows when the candle is burning. It can be used on its own as a method of decoration but is most attractive when combined with the three main decorating methods (i.e. painting, wax appliqué and pressed flowers).

Shapes can be cut out from a candle very simply by dipping the candle into the required colour of *Exterior* wax (90°C). After dipping the candle three times with 1 minute cooling time between dips, while the candle is still warm, cut out the required shape by pressing hard and pushing a cutter from left to right and up and down. (See pp. 42 and 43.)

Use a sharp knife to cut away the wax and lift out. You may then continue decorating by means of painting, wax appliqué, etc. or simply by following instructions for completing decorated candles.

Completing decorated candles

No matter what method of decoration was used, the following apply:

(a) Melt *Glossy Sealer* over low heat and when the temperature reaches 103°C hold candle by the wick (or by the stick if it is a candle on a stick) and dip gently but quickly into the *Glossy Sealer* wax. Wait 1 minute to cool and dip once more only. Should the candle be very big it will be easier to dip first the one half and then the other.

(b) If the candle needs levelling, you may use an old pan and level the candle over low heat. Trim the wick to 1 cm (3 cm for outdoor candles).

Angel's wings candles

These disc-shaped candles are called angel's wings because of the wings that are formed while the candle is burning, and are very simple to make. They must be supported at the bottom and because no suitable holders are available, one can use a piece of wood or bamboo that is flat on one side and has a slit in the other. I often use a cucumber for this purpose, slitting one side and cutting off a strip from the other side. You can also make holes in the cucumber with a toothpick and stick your favourite flowers into this 'base' (the flowers will stay fresh for a long time!).

Step 1
Over low heat melt together 2 parts *Interior* wax and 1 part *Exterior* wax (e.g. 500 g *Interior* and 250 g *Exterior*). Add colour chip and perfume and stir until dissolved.

Step 2
When wax reaches a temperature of 90°C, pour a thin layer into a lid or tart dish and leave to set.

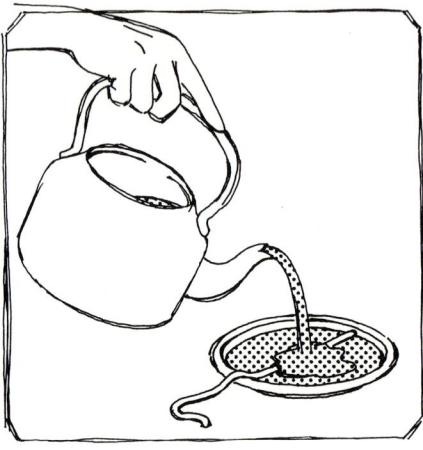

Step 3
When wax has set but is still warm to the touch, place a piece of wick across the centre and pour a thin layer of wax (90°C) over the wick. Leave to set and cool completely.

Step 4
Remove candle from the mould and dip into *Glossy Sealer* wax at 103°C. Wait 1 minute and dip once more. Trim wick to 1 cm.

N.B.
The contrasting colour on the borders of the angel's wings candles, pictured on page 7, is obtained by swirling wax of a contrasting colour around the edge of the lid or dish before proceeding to *Step 2*.

Layered candles

These very interesting candles are easy to make but because the wax has to be poured at fairly high temperatures, the moulds that can be used are limited to metal, only certain plastics, and ovenproof glass.

Step 1
Over low heat melt together 2 parts *Interior* wax and 1 part *Exterior* wax (e.g. 500 g *Interior* and 250 g *Exterior*).

Step 2
When wax has melted, divide the wax into three equal portions. Colour the wax by adding colour chips to each container. Try to work with complementary colours in either light, medium and dark shades or strong contrasts such as blue, red and yellow.

Step 3
Prepare the metal mould by following Steps 2(a), (b), (c) and (d) on page 28.

Step 4
Using the first colour pour a little wax into the mould (100°C). Leave to set but while wax is still warm, pour on the next colour (100°C). Once again allow to set but while still warm pour the third colour (100°C). Continue in this way until mould is filled to the brim. Leave to cool completely and remove as on page 28, *Step 4*.

Step 5
Dip candle into *Glossy Sealer* wax at 103°C, wait 1 minute to cool and dip once more.

Step 6
In an old pan over low heat, hold candle firmly and melt bottom level. Trim wick to 1 cm.

49

Sand and glue container candles

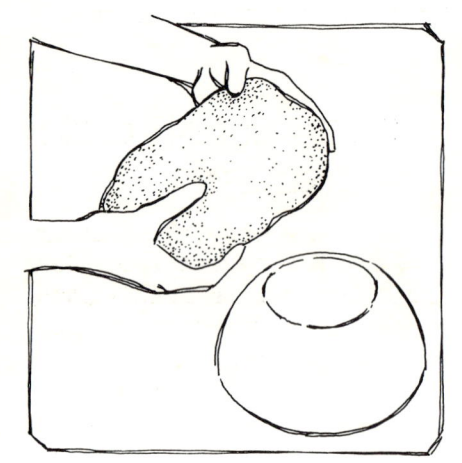

I thought of this method only as I was writing this book and I was thrilled with my discovery because of the possibilities of this sand and wall paper glue mixture. Examples pictured in this book are:

(a) Free-form sand and glue container candle (see picture on p. 7).
(b) Square sand and glue container candle with coloured layers of wax (see picture on p. 19).
(c) Sand and glue 'pebble' candles painted with poster paints (see picture on p. 15).
(d) Candle holder made of sand and glue for taper candles (see picture on p. 35).

To make the sand and wall paper glue mixture:
(1) Add 1,25 litres of water to 1 packet (60 gm) of wall paper glue and mix thoroughly until smooth (you may have to use an egg beater).
(2) Add clean sand (sandpit sand) and mix thoroughly until you have a pliable doughlike mixture.
(3) Work on trays covered with wax wrap so that you can easily remove the finished items.
(4) After you have made your sand and glue container by following the applicable instructions, this container must be left to dry either by being left in a shady spot for a couple of days or dried overnight in the oven (60°C).

Free-form sand and glue container candle

Select a dish or bowl. Grease the outside lightly with cooking oil and place upside down on a sheet of wax wrap. Flatten a large piece of the doughlike sand and glue mixture and lift it and lay over the bowl (see top sketch).
 Set aside to dry, remove bowl and fill with wax (see next page).

Square (or round)

Simply select a dish or bowl (glass or metal), grease inside with a little cooking oil and cover the inside by pressing the doughlike sand and glue mixture to the bottom and sides, trying to keep an even thickness. Set aside to dry, remove bowl and fill with wax as on the next page.

Sand and glue 'pebble' candles

Take a handful of the doughlike sand and glue mixture and press into a ball shape. Set aside on a sheet of wax wrap and using a kitchen knife, cut out from the middle of the ball either a square or circle and lift out this piece gently with the knife. Set aside to dry and fill with wax as on the next page. Paint this container using poster paints only after it has dried.

When the sand and glue containers are thoroughly dried, proceed as follows to fill them with wax:

Step 1
Melt over low heat 2 parts *Interior* wax and 1 part *Exterior* wax (e.g. 500 g *Interior* to 250 g *Exterior*) or if the candle is to be used outdoors, simply melt all scraps of wax.

Step 2
Prepare the sand and glue container by pouring a little of the melted wax (60°C) into it.

Step 3
(a) Cut a length of wick and press the end into the wax at the bottom of the container. Leave to cool completely.
(b) Tie the top of the wick to a sosatie stick and pour the wax (70°C) into the container leaving a little space at the top.
(c) Leave to cool completely and pour hot wax (100°C) to the brim of the container.

Step 4
When candle has cooled, trim wick to 1 cm for indoor use or 3 cm for outdoor use.

N.B. If you are going to use the candle outdoors, remember to use a triple wick instead of a single wick.

Candle holder for dipped tapered candles

This is easily made by putting the sand and glue mixture into a greased dessert bowl and pushing it down tightly. Holes are made with a stick pushed into the top. After drying this candle holder may be decorated with poster paints. The instructions for tapered candles are on page 32.

Coloured layers of wax inside the container

To achieve this effect simply pour a contrasting colour of wax (70°C) into the sand and glue container and swirl around the container. In this way build up a shell to the required thickness. You may use different colours of wax consecutively to make the shell multicoloured. Continue to fill the container by following *Steps 1–4* on the left.

Quick and easy sand candles for outdoor use

Melt all your scraps of wax (used candles and left-over wax) in a kettle. Take a bucket of slightly damp sand and using a bowl make an impression in the sand. Remove bowl gently.

Tie 3 pieces of wick to a block of wax and dip into melted wax to secure. Place this block of wax at the bottom of the sand impression and secure the wick by tying it to a stick which is placed horizontally over the bucket.

Pour the melted wax (120°C) into the sand impression over the block of wax, leaving a space at the top. Leave to cool completely and fill up the sand impression to the brim with wax at 120°C. Leave to cool completely, remove and trim wick to 3 cm.

Buyer's guide

- CNA stores countrywide for CRAFTYWAX basic candle-making kits.

- Craftywax Candle Making Clubs for all candle-making requirements as well as demonstrations and workshops.

    Contact

    Craftywax Advisory Service
    P.O. Box 13354
    Norkem Park 1631
    Tel. (011) 972-6072

- Craftywax Mail Orders for all candle-making requirements. Price lists are sent on request and all orders are sent promptly in the post.

    Write to Craftywax Mail Orders at the above address.

- Craftywax Wholesale Division for bulk supplies.

    Enquire at the above address.

- Supermarkets, hobby shops and stationery shops, as well as some florists' shops.

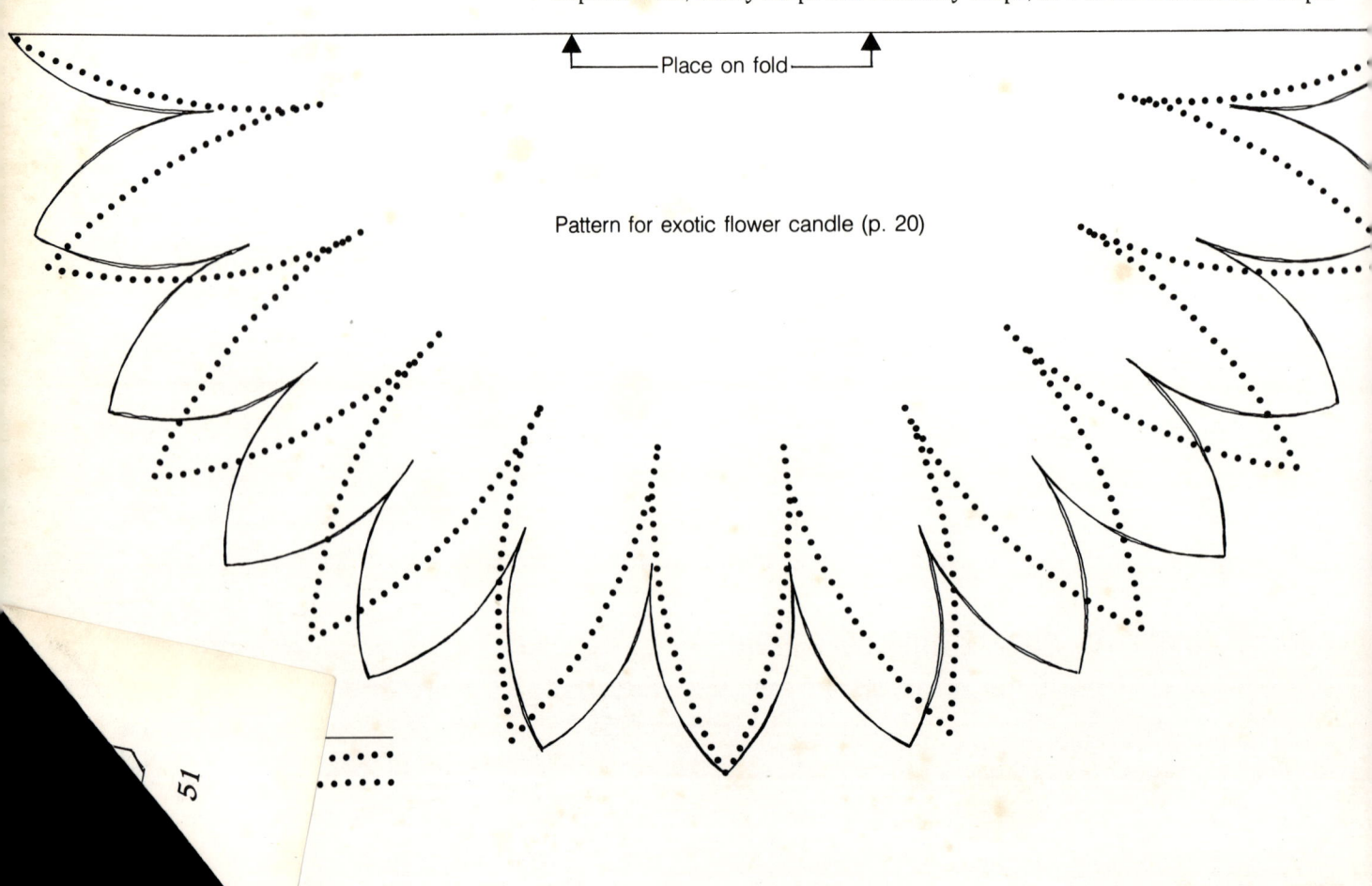

Place on fold

Pattern for exotic flower candle (p. 20)